# Love Your Patients!

**Scott Louis Diering, MD, MA**

Civilian Medical Officer
Dept. of Emergency Medicine
Walter Reed Army Medical Center
Washington, DC

Assistant Professor
Doctor of Medicine Program
International University of the Health Sciences
St. Kitts and Nevis — Dubai — India

Founder
Love Your Patients, Inc.
Frederick, Maryland

*Who are you? What are you? Where are you?*

Tell us your story! Are you a patient? A family member or friend of a patient? That's great ... tell us all about your experiences! We want to hear from you!

Are you a nurse? A doctor? A technician? An aide? Let us know about what your life in healthcare is like!

Email: stories@loveyourpatients.org

Phone the message line: 301 620 1933
or 1 866 227 8808 pin 7801

Mail it to us:　Love Your Patients!
　　　　　　　　99 Siegel Ct.
　　　　　　　　Frederick, Maryland 21702

Or visit our website, www.loveyourpatients.org
And go to the "Tell us about you!" section.

# Love Your Patients!

## Improving Patient Satisfaction with Essential Behaviors That Enrich the Lives of Patients and Professionals

SCOTT LOUIS DIERING, M.D.

Blue Dolphin Publishing

Published by Blue Dolphin Publishing, Inc.
P.O. Box 8, Nevada City, CA 95959
Orders: 1-800-643-0765
Web: www.bluedolphinpublishing.com

ISBN: 1-57733-141-9 softcover
ISBN: 1-57733-159-1 hardcover


Library of Congress Cataloging-in-Publication Data

Diering, Scott Louis, 1961-
  Love your patients! : essential behaviors that enrich the lives of
patients and caregivers / Scott Louis Diering.
      p. ; cm.
  Includes bibliographical references and index.
  ISBN 1-57733-141-9 (pbk. : alk. paper)
  1. Medical personnel and patient.
  [DNLM: 1. Professional-Patient Relations. 2. Caregivers—
psychology. 3. Empathy. 4. Patient Care—psychology. W 21.5
D563L 2004] I. Title.

  R727.3.D53 2004
  610.69'6—dc22

                                                    2004007015

Printed in the United States of America

10    9    8    7    6    5    4    3

# Contents

# Acknowledgments

First, I must thank all the patients for whom I have ever cared. Each one has taught me more than I will ever know.

Equally importantly, I must thank all my fellow care-givers, especially the nurses, with whom I have ever worked. Without each and every one of you, as role models, this would have been very difficult to write.

I thank Dr. Robert Mallin, who provided vast amounts of time and energy offering editorial counsel and the wisdom of his experience.

I thank Dr. Mary Peterson, Ms. Suzanne Poynter, and Social Worker Shelly Fales, who each provided me with strong support, and encouragement.

I thank Ms. Roxanne Thompson and Ms. Bobbi Thompson, who shared their brilliance, their experience and their command of the English language.

I thank Ms. Diana Fox, RN, who provided me with cheerfulness in the face of despair, and who reminds everyone what agape means.

Most importantly, I thank Ms. Sandy Reitz from the depths of my soul. She offers continuous, unconditional support, and, as executive director of Love Your Patients!, Inc., is instrumental in helping share the Love.

I thank Dr. Martin Groder. His suggestions led to the inception of Love Your Patients!, and his wisdom has forever changed my life. Thanks, Marty.

# What's Love
# Got to Do with It?

# 1

# Introduction: What's This All About?

*"Love is an act of will—*
*namely, both an intention and an action."*
—M. Scott Peck

What is this book anyway, some kind of touchy-feely new age handbook? Who is this author, some kind of self-proclaimed prophet? Who does he think we are, a bunch of heartless robots, who need to learn about feelings? Is this guy trying to fix healthcare with some finger-wagging guilt sermon?

No, no, no, no.

I am a physician. I practice emergency medicine. I see lots of patients. And I have discovered, through trial and error, as well as by reading the literature, that our behaviors, our *attitudes*, have a profound impact on our patients. Every one of them.

This book is full of reminders. Reminders on how to be nice, so our patients get better faster. Reminders on what we can *say*, so our patients stay better. Reminders on what we can *do*, so our patients don't sue us. Reminders on how to *act*, so our patients tell our boss that we are great. The purpose of this book is to organize some of these reminders, and lay them out so they are easy to remember, while we are at work.

Our job in healthcare today is a lot harder than it has ever been before, and it looks like it's only going to get harder. It seems that we are always caring for more patients, who are sicker, with less help, while we work longer hours. You know the drill. Just one more.... .

I wrote this book to make our jobs easier, and at the same time, to make our patients happier. I have tried to make it easy to read, and easy to remember. I hope you enjoy it.

And, I hope your patients enjoy it, too.

To begin, let's review the story of Ms. Case.

## Ms. Case's Weakness

"This isn't happening," Ms. Case thought to herself. "This can't be happening. It's all a dream."

Ms. Cindy Case lay on the stretcher. She is naked except for a sheet covering her. Her clothes are cut off and on the floor. She is in a resuscitation room at the trauma center. She is staring up at the ceiling. She doesn't remember the accident that brought her here.

The staff's excitement at her arrival has evaporated. She is stable. She has had her chest, pelvis and cervical spine X-rayed. She has been to the CT scanner and back. She has two large-bore IVs, a Foley catheter in her bladder, and an NG tube through her nose and into her stomach.[1] The floor is a mess of sterile wrappers and IV fluids. But Ms. Case can't see the mess. She can't move. She is paralyzed. She is now a quadriplegic.[2]

---

[1] Standard trauma resuscitation includes IV fluids which can be given rapidly ("large bore," usually 16 or 18 gauge, peripheral), a bladder catheter and naso-gastric tube to suction.

[2] Quadriplegic: Profound weakness of all four extremities (arms and legs).

"What's happening to me?" She cries out. Her mouth is dry and thick with old blood. She can't feel her hands or her feet. She tries to look around, but she can't move her head because of the bulky C-collar.[3] Terror and panic begin to smother her. Nurse Malouf starts to come toward her, just as a doctor enters the room.

The nurse's attention immediately shifts from Ms. Case to Dr. Flemm.

"She's a quad," says the nurse. "The trauma surgeon is in with a gunshot next door. He told me to tell you her CT is done."

"What level?" asks Dr. Flemm.

"C5."[4]

"No," he says, with some disbelief.

"Yeah, watch. Ms. Case, shrug your shoulders."

Ms. Case struggled, but she could bring her shoulders up a little, despite the C-collar. She bent her elbows a little, too.

"See? Now watch."

"Ms. Case, squeeze my fingers."

Ms. Case struggled as hard as she could, but her fingers would not move. Her eyes begged for some reassurance from the people staring at her.

She began to cry. "What's happening to me? Why can't I move my fingers?" She imagined trying to feed her baby at home without her arms.

"Ms. Case, you've been in an accident," Nurse Malouf said. "You are badly injured. This is the neurosurgeon. He has some questions."

"Can you feel this?" Dr. Flemm was sticking her chest with the sharp end of a broken wooden Q-tip.

---

[3] C-collar or cervical spine collar. This stabilizes a patient's neck (or cervical spine) and is applied at the scene by paramedics for most accident victims.

[4] A patient's level of motor function (best assessed after 24 hours) that correlates with the vertebral (spinal) nerve root level.

"Are you touching me?" asks Ms. Case, with panic in her voice.

Then, Dr. Flemm stuck her just below her clavicle.[5]

Ms. Case says, with desperate hope in her voice, "Yes, ouch, I can feel that!"

"Can you feel this?" asks Dr. Flemm. He uses the bottom of his pen to stroke the sole of her foot. As he does this, there is no movement.

"Feel what?" She starts to panic again. Her eyes searching the faces of the nurse and the doctor for ... anything. Nothing was there.

"Yeah, she's a quad all right. I'll go look at the scan. Get her to the ICU. I'll check her bulbocavernosus[6] up there. She on pressors?"[7] he asked as he examined her IV fluids. "No? Good. No shock. Good. She'll probably need a stabilization procedure, not that it'll do much good," he mused aloud, while he wrote some orders.

"What?" yelled Ms. Case. "It has to do good!"

"I can't move!" cried Ms. Case. "Please, do something! Help me!"

She was crying loudly. Nurse Malouf was picking pieces of glass out of her hair.

"Third one so far this year. Too bad," said Dr. Flemm.

Ms. Case sobbed.

\* \* \* \* \*

---

[5] Clavicle: Collar bone, the only boney attachment of the upper extremity to the axial skeleton.

[6] Bulbocavernosus: Reflex, which, if present, suggests incomplete spinal cord injury; tested by placing examiner's finger in the rectum and feeling for anal contraction when gentle traction is placed on the Foley catheter.

[7] Pressors: Vasopressor drugs, which raise blood pressure, often used for patients suffering from true neurogenic shock.

How was Ms. Case's care?

Great, we might say. She was treated in a trauma center. She was stabilized. She had her IV lines, catheters, X-rays done. She is going to be scheduled for surgery. She will survive. Isn't that enough?

No! That is not enough! Ms. Case has one of the worst possible injuries a person can have! She is suffering some of the most terrible anguish a person can go through. And her caregivers do not seem to care.

Although excellent *technical* care was provided, Ms. Case needs more than that. She desperately needs some love. I hope you agree that Dr. Flemm and Nurse Malouf do not really *care*, although they provide adequate medical care. While their technical skills may be good, they are entirely too unemotional and uncaring.

Ms. Case's story should panic us. As we feel her terror, her confusion, her agony, we should want to help her, comfort her, console her. We are probably disgusted with Nurse Malouf and Dr. Flemm, and the whole trauma center. We want to help Ms. Case.

What would you do if you were caring for Ms. Case?

By the time you finish this book, you will have *many* good ways to help Ms. Case and her family, while providing your excellent healthcare.

Now, don't fret. Not all the sample patient stories are this depressing. We discuss Ms. Case to remind us that *quality* care is more than excellent *technical* care. Good healthcare can only be delivered when we treat each patient as a *person*, not just some disease or complaint or injury.

### What's in It for You?

This book can help you be even better at what you do.

After you assimilate some of these guidelines, you will be more satisfied with your job. There will be more fulfillment in your life. You will be happier. You will see your potential for greatness.

When you practice some of these ideas, you will be better able to do your job. Your delivery of healthcare will be easier, more enjoyable and more accurate. You will deftly discover what other people need, as well as what you can do to help.

When you apply these skills, your patients will be happier, more satisfied and they will tell your boss how good you are. Your hospital or office or clinic will become a great place to visit, and it will be because of you.

You and your employer will be less likely to get sued.

### How Does *Love Your Patients!* Work?

This book is full of reminders. In this first section, we discuss very specific actions—actions which show our patients that we really care about them. We will review these actions in the next several chapters. Each action falls into a category. The categories are compassion, respect and humility. These actions equal love, *agape* love.

In the middle section, there are more patient stories. These stories are about patients and their caregivers, caregivers that do not act with love. After each story, we will critique each caregiver. Then, I will suggest tips and techniques for you to use at work. Hopefully, you'll find these reminders simple, pleasant and enjoyable to practice.

This information is distilled from my own experience, as well as the experience of many loving caregivers with whom I have worked. These experiences are strongly supported by the literature. In the last section, I review specific studies which further support these ideas.

I'm sure you will find it easy and rewarding to practice love at work. You will make healthcare better for everyone.

Who should read this book? Everyone who cares for other people! In fact, let's discuss who is a caregiver and who is a patient.

**Summary: Caring for patients involves more than just delivering technical interventions for their problem.** *Love Your Patients!* **can help you enjoy your job, while you do it better.**

# Who Are We?
# Caregivers and Patients

*"I'd rather know what type of a person has a disease
than what disease a person has."*
—Sir William Osler

Who is a patient? Who is a caregiver? Can someone be both at the same time?

It is helpful for us to have very broad definitions of these roles. That way, no one is left out.

## Caregivers

Who is a caregiver? A caregiver is *any* person who may interact with a patient (or the patient's family) while the patient has any needs or concerns. Anyone.

Traditionally, we think of caregivers as nurses and doctors. However, in the office, clinic or hospital setting, *every person* with whom a patient may have contact is a caregiver. It does not matter what we do—security, pharmacy, housekeeping, reception clerk—if we have contact with patients, we are caregivers.

How can this be? *We* have the ability to impact a patient. *We* can set the tone for the whole patient encounter. *We* may need to touch a frightened patient, a naked patient, or a lost patient. Therefore, we are caregivers. No one is exempt. To our patients, we are *all* caregivers.

For example, I was once in a hospital where a confused, elderly inpatient slipped past the nurse's station and began to wander around the hospital. She wandered through radiology, past the cafeteria, and through the lobby. She passed at least fifty hospital employees, including doctors, nurses, techs, everyone. No one recognized her, so no one said anything. Finally, on her way out to the parking deck, a volunteer asked her if she needed help. The patient was slow to respond, so the volunteer checked her ID bracelet, and brought her back to her room. They got back just as the elopement alert was being given. That volunteer may have saved the patient's life, and she certainly saved someone's job. No one else who she wandered past noticed her at all. We can almost hear all those caregivers saying, "Not my patient, not my job." But this isn't true. We are all caregivers, for each and every patient.

We, as caregivers, have a unique responsibility in this world. We have the privilege of helping people who need help the most.

As caregivers, we are all in this thing called "healthcare" together. In this book, we minimize the distinctions between doctors, nurses, technicians, assistants, etc., because we are all caregivers. Every one of us is in the health-caring profession. After all, our goal is all the same: Provide excellent care, the best we can provide, for each and every patient.

When we love our job, and love our patients, providing excellent care is a lot easier.

"Why make a big deal out of it?" someone might say, "It's nothing special. Just go in, slap a little healthcare on 'em, get the job done, and get out. Nobody loves me, why should I love them back?"

This type of thinking is toxic. This thinking is toxic because healthcare is *very* special. In no other job are we given instant intimacy with another person. We are exposed to hurt, sick, dying, unhappy people all the time. And all of them, silently or loudly, call for our help.

The amazing thing is, we *can* help. We can make a huge difference in another person's life. We may not cure their cancer, or bring their baby back to life, or reverse their Alzheimer's. However, we can touch them, comfort them, and make a *difference*. With just a little love, we can make their suffering more tolerable.

And, we will be happier for it.

## Patients

Who, then, is the patient?

You might say, "Obviously, it's the sick one, the one lying in the bed. Can't you see? How did you get through medical school, anyway?"

While the patient *is* the sick person, "the patient" is much more than the *one* sick person. "The patient" is also any family member who is worried about their loved one. "The patient" is visitors, clergy and everyone else who has an interest in that sick person.

"The patient" may not be sick at all. "The patient" is any person in need, any person worried about their health, or any person who seeks information about wellness or diseases or symptoms.

"The patient" includes a huge number of people, usually with one sick person at the center. Anyone who is concerned about *that* sick person is a patient. Great Aunt Mabel in Oshkosh, Nebraska who calls you up at three in the morning to check on her niece who just had arthroscopic[1] knee surgery is your patient. The police officer investigating an impaired driver involved in a motor vehicle accident is your patient. The social worker investigating a case of domestic abuse is both a caregiver *and* a patient.

It is so much easier to include all these persons as "patients." It reminds us that our principles of providing healthcare apply to anyone. Everyone we encounter at work is *either* a patient or a caregiver!

This broad view of who is a patient is very handy. For example, I have had the pleasure of making television and radio information spots for a hospital where I once worked. These "Medical Minutes" were broadcast locally, and gave general information on various health topics. While I was making these segments, the entire local population was my patient! However, we don't have to make TV spots to have this broad view! *Everyone* may be our patient! This way, we won't miss anyone who may need our care.

Now, let us discuss what is love, that is, caregiver love.

**Summary: Anyone with any interest in an ill person, or with any questions about health or disease, is a patient. Anyone who may contact a patient is a caregiver.**

---

[1] Arthroscopic: Minimally invasive surgery of a joint through small incisions, using cameras.

# *Love, Caregiver Style*

> *"I think one's feelings waste themselves in words;*
> *they ought all to be distilled into actions,*
> *and into actions which bring results."*
> —Florence Nightingale

"Love? Why love?" you might ask. "Why not 'Admire Your Patients,' or 'Appreciate Your Patients'?"

Why love? Because love is big. Very big. It has huge potential to improve our lives, and the lives of our patients.

It's true that "love" is one of the most abused words in the English language. However, there is tremendous power in a pure, unselfish love.

Our love, caregiver love, is unique. This type of love is not a feeling—it's an action. Caregiver love is *observed* through our actions. Here, and in the next three chapters, we will discuss the specific actions that we, the caregivers, show when we demonstrate love. Showing love to our patients is good for them, and good for us.

### Love, Agape Style

The word "love" is too vague and too broad. We need to distinguish caregiver love from the love of romance novels and TV commercials. For us, as healthcare workers, *agape* best describes this type of love.

Agape is from ancient Greek. Now remember, the ancient Greeks had several different words for "love." *Eros, philos,* and *agape* are distinct aspects of love. While *eros* is romantic and passionate love, and *philos* is brotherly love, *agape* is most relevant for us, the caregivers. Agape refers to love of all humanity. It is a sincere caring for all humans.

(If you wish to read more on this topic, an excellent resource is the book *Agape Love*, by Sir John Templeton. In it, he tells us, "Agape love is a practice of goodwill, kindness, forgiveness and compassion to others." He describes how agape love is universal.)

Agape, the deep spiritual love, the love of empathy and understanding, the love of openness and interest, the love of caring and compassion, is something everyone needs to feel, *especially* our patients. When they feel loved, we have started them on a critical step in getting better.

Agape is perfect for us in the health fields. In order for our patients to feel the *caring* component of health*care*, they need to feel loved. Agape is the love that we, the caregivers, have for our patients. Without agape, we are no better than Nurse Malouf or Dr. Flemm.

"Wait a minute!" you might say, "I don't love anybody! I just take care of sick people, that's all!"

Fine. It does not really matter how we *feel*. It is more important that we *act* in a loving manner. The feeling of unconditional love will follow our actions, the actions that show love.

### The Big Three: Compassion, Respect, Humility

Agape, or caregiver love, exists when we behave with compassion, respect and humility. Each of these qualities arises from different parts of us.

Compassion is a manifestation of love from our heart. Respect is love from our spirit. Humility is how we show love from our mind, or our intellect.

Agape, or caregiver love, is not accidental. Showing compassion, respect and humility requires purposeful, intentional actions.

Everything we do or say impacts our patients. For example, when a patient calls up and says,

"My stomach hurts so badly!"

We can say,

"OK, let me get some more information..."

Or, we can say,

"I'm sorry, before we can help, I need to get some more information...."

Can you *feel* the difference between those two responses? The second response doesn't take any more time or energy to say, but it makes a huge difference to the patient on the other end. With the second response, the patient knows that someone cares.

Cushioning our words and our actions with the soft warmth of agape is easy. Compassion and respect and humility are the fuels that fire the warmth of agape. Agape allows us to truly impact the patient's visit, or their illness, or their life, with as little as a smile or greeting.

Agape is never *instead* of a patient's medical care. Agape is offered *at the same time* that we provide the standard healthcare. Our actions, made gentle and sweet with our compassion, respect and humility, give flavor, color and vibrancy to the otherwise sterile delivery of healthcare.

By sharing agape love with a patient, we nourish and minister to them in a way different from any medicine or surgery.

**Healthcare: It's More Than a Job…**

It's easy for us to forget the incredible jobs that we have. Patients expose their souls, and their bodies, to us. We hear their prayers and dreams and hopes. We hear things like,

"I think I might have HIV," or

"My husband has been urinating in the houseplants," or

"I took all my pills because I wish I were dead."

Like it or not, we are instant insiders in our patient's lives. This goes *way beyond* a job.

Does agape love seem like too much too handle? "Why can't we just do our job, provide our service, take care of them, and get out?" Well, we can, but then we will be hollow, and our patients might not get better. We will be more like Dr. Flemm or Nurse Malouf than a loving caregiver.

It's like this: We go to work, right? We are caring for patients anyway, right? Then why not do our job so our patients feel better about their visit? Then *we* will feel better about our selves. Further, with agape, we will decrease the likelihood that we will be sued, or fired or not promoted. There's no reason *not* to behave with agape!

We are all in this thing called healthcare together. All of us, doctors, nurses, technicians, assistants, can benefit from agape. Our goals are all the same: Provide excellent care, the best we can provide, for each and every patient. When we love our patients, providing excellent care is a lot easier.

Agape, our deep unselfish love, the love of insight and concern, the love from our reverence for life, is something we all need. When patients feel loved, we have given them crucial help towards getting better.

## What Goes Around, Comes Around

When our patients experience our love, they will be better patients: better historians, more honest, more cooperative and more open to our suggestions. This is true regardless of what role we play in their care.

As we cultivate our love for each of our patients, the helpful things we can do for them will blossom before our eyes. Our patient's secondary gains, hidden agendas, real needs, and barriers to healing will be revealed. We will listen with increased attention and acuity. We will care, and they will know it.

There is a nice side effect to agape. By demonstrating love for our patients, we will *glow* in their eyes. They will feel better than they have felt in a long time, and they'll attribute their well-being to us. Gradually, we will improve our ability to read people, we will become more intuitive, and people will like us more. As we get better at sharing agape love with others around us, we will feel a vast improvement in *our* quality of life. Our potential for greatness will open up before us.

When our work glows after it is polished with love, not only will we have gotten the job done, but also people around us will feel our shine. We will stand out just a little bit more. We will be appreciated.

Acting with agape does not really change anyone's interpersonal style. Instead, agape gives us some reminders, or tools, which we can use to make our care-giving more enjoyable. Some of these ideas will seem natural to us; others will take some energy and practice. However, over time, agape makes our job easier. With agape, there are fewer ugly interactions with noncompliant and problem patients. There is less time spent debating which competing therapies will work best. We can enjoy a mutually beneficial visit from all our patients. Soon, our patients will love us, too.

## Objections?

> *"The opposite of love is not hate ... it is indifference."*
> —Eli Weisel

You might say, "Love my patients? I can't even stand them, they are nothing but a bunch of whiney, demanding ingrates, who never do what I ask and get healthy more to spite me than to please me!" If you think like this, as many of us have at one time or another, you are either in the wrong profession, or desperately in need of some coaching. Agape will help.

The privilege of providing healthcare is a calling. It's a *vocation*, beyond just a job. Yet, the stress and pace of modern medicine can be overwhelming for us, the caregivers. These reminders will help us all keep sight of the important things, while showing our patients that we care.

A good goal is to be better caregivers. It does not matter if we are a doctor who is chief of surgery at a university medical center or if we are a nurse's aide in a nursing home. If we interact with patients, we will do a better job with agape. By demonstrating love for our patients, we will be more helpful and more powerful. People will notice our caring and loving attitude. We will go a long way to making the world a better place.

Did Nurse Malouf or Dr. Flemm behave lovingly to Ms. Case? No. Technically speaking, care was provided. No gross negligence occurred. There was no major deviation from the standard of care. However, this is a lousy standard.

You realized that something in Ms. Case's care was missing.... Something big was missing from the interaction. In fact, several big things were missing: compassion, respect, and humility. Love was missing.

In the next three chapters, I provide practical, useful definitions for *compassion, respect* and *humility*. Your job is to choose those actions which best suit you. Use these reminders to polish and buff up your usual routine.

It's hard to be loving in the midst of crying patients and beepers and heart tones and paperwork (gag!). So these tools are easy to remember. I will suggest more reminders than you will need, so pick out which actions you tend to forget or leave out while at work, and try to blend those into your current caregiving style. Later, you can apply those behaviors that you find most challenging.

This book doesn't teach anyone how to practice medicine, nursing, or any other allied health skill. This is all *style*.

Let us now look at some of the actions that define our caregiver love, that is, agape.

Summary: As caregivers, we have an amazing ability to impact our patients. Agape is the type of unconditional love that we have for our patients. We show agape when we act with compassion, respect and humility.

# Compassion: Love from Our Heart

*"If you want others to be happy, practice compassion.*
*If you want to be happy, practice compassion."*
—Dalai Lama

Compassion comes from our heart. It is the most important attribute that separates us, as caregivers, from machines. If we lack compassion, we might work in healthcare, but we are not *care*givers.

The dictionary has a two-part definition of compassion. Compassion is "sympathetic consciousness of others' distress together with a desire to alleviate it." Compassion is a *feeling* (the sympathy for another's distress) *and* an *action* (wanting to help alleviate that distress). As caregivers, we are conscious of our patient's distress *and* we help them out of their distress.

Compassion is both a feeling *and* an action. For now, the feeling of compassion is not important. The feeling will come later. However, our actions should definitely *show* compassion. If we want our patients to experience compassionate care, we must *demonstrate* compassion by our actions.

Compassion is at the core of being a caregiver. When our patients experience our compassionate care, they know that they are not alone in their pain. *Showing* compassion is so important, that we should show our compassion on three different levels. When we show compassion on the emotional level, this is **empathy**. When we show compassion on the interpersonal level, we **minister** to our patients. And, when we show compassion on the intellectual level, we pay **attention** to our patients.

### Empathy: "I can imagine what you must be feeling..."

*"I was fortunate to have as a physician a man who was able to put himself in the position of the patient."*
—Norman Cousins, *Anatomy of an Illness*

Empathy is compassion on the emotional level. Empathy is the ability to feel what another person feels. Empathy means that our patient's hurt or pain or sadness has touched us, touched us deeply inside our being. We are so aware of *their* feelings that we can almost feel those feelings ourself.

When we empathize, we don't literally "feel their pain." Instead, empathy is our understanding of what it must be like to feel what they feel. But, for empathy to have any meaning, we have to *show* that we can imagine what they feel.

Many papers and books have been written about empathy. (See, e.g., Spiro et al, *Empathy and the Practice of Medicine*, 1993.) However, there's no reason to make this complex. Let's keep it simple. Here are three steps that demonstrate empathy:

1. **Look, listen, feel;**
2. **Acknowledge** what your patient shares; and
3. **Use facial expressions.**

*Look, Listen, Feel*

The first step to empathy is to read your patient. When we accurately read another person, we know (or guess) what they are feeling inside of them. We can then bring that feeling inside of us. That way, we can know what it is like to be living what they are living.

To read someone, we must be willing to integrate their *words* with their *tone of voice*, their *facial expressions* and their *body language*. This takes a little practice but becomes easy once we allow ourselves to do it.

Interpreting pain-complaints is a good way to work on empathy skills. For example, when I practiced in western Nebraska, I treated a lot of cowboys and rodeo riders. I had one patient with an obvious shoulder dislocation. He was sweating, gripping the stretcher, and almost crying. I said, "I think you need some pain medications, before X rays." He replied, through gritted teeth, gasping, "No doc, it's okay, it don't hurt too much."

Here was a critical choice-point. Do I believe his *words* ("No doc, its okay…") or his *actions and expressions* (sweating, holding on to the stretcher, etc.), which said he was in a lot of pain?

I chose to read the obvious clues he was giving me. I explained to him, "This type of injury usually hurts a lot. Even though you are not hurting too badly, *I* would feel better if I could give you some pain medicine." He agreed to an IV, and accepted the morphine. "OK, doc," he winced, "But just for you." We both felt a lot better.

I *chose* to empathize with this patient. I could have accepted his verbal statement, documented his refusal of pain medication, and sent him to X-ray. However, this would not have been good care. I empathized. I read his non-verbal cues, and acted on those cues by explaining what would make *me* feel better. I never asked my patient to admit he was in pain, nor did I explain to him he did not need to appear macho in an ER. I told him how I felt, and I asked him if *he* would make *me* feel better.

Although his *pain* was a key part of my empathy, I also empathized with his need to be tough and refuse pain medications. I could relate to his pain.... I could almost feel his pain in his look and posture. At the same time, I could sense his need to be tough, and his desire to not cry and not beg for relief. I would never have given him pain medications if he continued to refuse them: It's his right to refuse. But I understood him, and he understood me, and together we agreed on a management course that benefited both of us.

When we read our patients, our patients are very grateful. They sense that we understand them, because our responses are very accurate, and appropriate to what they feel deep down inside.

There are several very good research articles on this topic of picking up on clues. For example, Levinson, et al (2000) analyzes a huge number of patient-doctor interactions. These authors identify the clues that the patients give their doctors about what's really important. Sometimes the docs pick up on the clues; other times they ignore the clues. If a doc picks up on clues and responds to those clues, the patients are much happier.

The pitfall here is to avoid *projecting* our values onto our patients. As we talk with our patients, we need to be aware of *our* goals and agendas. No patient wants *our* opinions jammed down their throat. Instead, we just listen, and feel, and read what they offer us.

When we do this, the most amazing things happen. When we tune into our patients, and figure out where they are coming from, we develop a sense of mercy. We are not able to be angry with them for their imperfections. We accept each patient and work with them, without criticism or judgments. Then, we become a sort of "patient-advocate." We've achieved this level of care-giving when we defend our patients against criticisms or complaints.

Detractors might say that empathy is bad. By empathizing, caregivers take on too much emotional burden, and later these caregivers are overwhelmed by other people's emotional problems.

This is false. Emotions need to be exercised too. Emotions are like every other part of us: Use it or lose it. The more we *feel* for other people, the less callous and less hardened we become. Remember, when we accept part of our patient's pain via empathy, we reduce their pain. However, *we* can then leave that pain outside their door. We do not have to carry it home.

If we choose to build up emotional callouses in our soul, we may be better able to distance our self from the pain other people suffer, but we will also distance our self from their joys and happiness, too.

### *R.S.V.P. (Respond, please!)*

A second step in empathizing with the patient is to *respond to* their anguish. *Reading* a patient's pain signals or clues is not enough. We must let our patients *know* that we hear them.

Pain is a common complaint. Sometimes we can offer help in relieving it, sometimes we are causing it, and other times it is a sign of a bigger problem. The source and importance of the pain can be put aside for the few seconds it takes to show that we *recognize* their pain. For example, we can acknowledge their suffering with phrases like,

"I am sorry, *that must be awful for you…*"

"*I know this hurts,* and I am sorry, but please bear with me for one more minute..."

"I hear you, and *I know it's hard for you...*"

"*I understand* what you must be going through..."

Statements like these prove to our patients that we grasp their experience. It's very important to let our patients know that we *do* suffer with them. They will feel better for it. The key is that they are *not alone* in their difficult time. This is the benefit of empathy. A shared burden is much easier to carry. For patients who may not want to burden their family, sharing the burden of their anxieties and pain with a caregiver is an immense relief.

Pain is not the only distress with which we can empathize. The emotional anguish of families, the fear of dying, and the confusion surrounding complex medical care are all very upsetting experiences that we can share.

One of the most overlooked opportunities to show our compassion is when we ask about a patient's family history. When a person mentions that their parent died, we can say, "I'm sorry..." or "Oh, that must be hard..." before we ask details about how or when they died. We show them that we feel their pain, and that it's painful to bring up the death of a loved one.

You might ask, "What do I actually *do* to let someone know I empathize?" It's easy. **Nod your head,** and **move your hands.** A lot. There are good research papers on patient satisfaction saying we need to physically move (by nodding our heads and moving our hands) in order for our empathy to be believed (Sherer & Rogers, 1980; Mehrabian & Williams, 1969).

Allow yourself to appear dramatic! Wave your arms around and bob your head up and down when you empathize! Your patients will love you for it!

So, if we are unsure of our empathy-demonstrating behaviors: We can nod our head a lot and move our hands a lot.

*Face Facts*

We also show empathy via our facial expressions. The ability to communicate through facial expressions is very important. Our patients will know what's in our heart from the expression that's on our face. Even more than our vocal tones and inflections, our faces reveal our true feelings.

Therefore, make faces! When our patients are sharing sad stories, we must wrinkle our brows and show our sadness on our faces. When they are proud of an accomplishment, we smile with them, while we praise them. When they make a joke, we laugh with them.

Our face must match our words. While a smile is perhaps the most universal facial expression, it should not be our only facial expression. So, when our patients tell us about their discomfort or pain, we must show in our face that we care… Furrowed brows, turned down mouth, or lifted eyebrows… anything to show that we are reacting to what they said.

Studies have shown that it is very frustrating to speak with someone who does not reveal any facial expressions (Giannini et al, 1984). Nobody likes interacting with a deadpan, emotionless person. Nobody likes a human robot.

Suppose we don't know what type of facial expression is appropriate? What if we can't figure out what our patient is feeling, or we just don't express our self well? Then, make the face that they make. Mirror them. When we reflect back what we see on their face, they will see that we can feel what they are feeling. And, via proprioceptive and kinesthetic[1] feedback, we will actually feel some of the emotions that they feel (Levenson, Ekman & Friesen, 1990)!

---

[1] Proprioceptive and kinesthetic: Sensory inputs giving us touch and position sense.

Our face will reveal what is in our heart. If we present a bored or apathetic face to our patient, they will know we do not really care (King et al, 1983). We must never even hint boredom, or disbelief or apathy on our faces. To do so is to transmit the worst possible message: We don't care.

We should always show our love on our face.

## Minister: "I care about you."

> *"It's not how much we give, but how much love we put in the doing—That's compassion in action."*
> —Mother Teresa

Compassion on the interpersonal level is ministering. We minister when we do our job *and* show that we care. Caring is part of compassion. After all, we are health*care* workers. We *care* about other people.

Ministering describes the *way* we deliver our healthcare … its style points. Ministering is the attitude of caring and concern that patients want.

How do we minister? We minister when we **comfort** our patients, when we **get close** and **touch** them, and when we use "**I**" statements.

### Be Supportive and Comforting

A huge part of ministering is comforting. When we see that someone is in pain or anguish or worry, we try to help. They know they are not alone.

We don't have to know *what* is bothering someone to comfort them. We just have to acknowledge that something is wrong, and softly and gently let them know we are available for them.

Sometimes comforting means telling our patient, "Don't worry…." However, it is crucial that we never appear dismissive. We must treat every concern, every worry, with sincere interest and importance. *Nothing* is trivial.

Comforting may involve a deeper relationship. Our patient may believe that we are the only one in the world who actually cares about them, who cares about what happens to them. This belief in our caring is very comforting to them, and may be enough to carry them through their illness.

I recall caring for an elderly woman who was having an MI.[2] She was in terrible pain. We gave her nitroglycerine, aspirin, morphine, and we finally got her pain under control. However, she was still very upset. She refused to stay in the hospital. When I asked why she wanted to go home, she looked at me, and, with tears in her eyes, she explained that there was no one to take care of her little dog. I held her hands and promised her that we'd find someone who'd feed and walk her dog. She cried with relief, and agreed to stay.

Had I not tried to comfort her, I might have never found out why she wanted to leave. I could have let her sign out AMA,[3] and let her go. Fortunately, she did fine. Her little dog did fine, too.

We can use any opportunity we have to be comforting. For example, when gathering a medical history, we show we care by injecting some compassionate words. When someone tells us they lost their job, we say, "*I'm so sorry* ... that must be hard." If our patient says they're having terrible pain, before we explore the *PQRST,*[4] we say, "I'm sorry, tell me more about it... ," or "Oh my gosh, how long?... ," or "You must be very strong to tolerate that...." Our patients

---

[2] MI: Myocardial infarction or heart attack.

[3] AMA: Against Medical Advice, that is, when a patient refuses the suggested care.

[4] Position, Quality, Relationships & Radiations, Severity, Timing of any pain complaints.

need to know that we care about their suffering as much as we do about the details of their medical history.

There is a great nursing article on this. JM Morse (2000) reviews the topic quite eloquently in her article, "On Comfort and Comforting." She discusses technical aspects of comforting, as well as some specific behaviors that comfort.

## Get a Little Closer

The privilege of touching our patients distinguishes health care from just about all other professions. When was the last time the check-out clerk at your supermarket held your hand when she asked, "Did you find everything you were looking for?" Or your computer troubleshooter put their arm around you when they explained why your computer locked up? Only at *our* work do we *touch* our customers as a part of the job.

Again, it's style points. *How* we touch our patients makes the difference. Ministering to patients requires a soft touch. A two-handed greeting, a gentle hand on the shoulder when auscultating,[5] or hand on their foot while we stand at the bedside, establishes a connection of compassion that is tangible to them. It's real. For our frightened, older patients, we can hold their hand gently while we talk. This helps them relax.

Every time we touch someone, it should be a special touch, a customized touch, just for that patient. One touch does not fit all. The tough young man will need a very different type of touch from the infant in its mother's arms. Either way, our touch is a very important part of our healing.

Some patients come to us just so they *will* be touched. They may live alone, or have a mental illness or just be lonely.

---

[5] Auscultate: Listening to the body's sounds, usually with a stethoscope, to diagnose.

If we fail to make contact with them, above and beyond our stethoscope or blood pressure cuff, they will leave unfulfilled. They will seek a different provider who *will* touch them. No one wants to believe that they are a pariah, or untouchable. Please, we should never let our patients think that they are not worthy of our touch.

A psychologist I once worked with felt that human contact is a *nutritive requirement*. He claims that physical health depends, in part, upon adequate doses of caring touch. There is good scientific evidence to support this (see, e.g., Dingman et al, 1999).

Suppose we don't have time to touch someone, or it just would not fit. For example, a mental health visit, or a quick follow up. In these cases, moving a little bit closer may be enough. Research has shown that patients rate their caregivers highly if the caregivers lean forward and get a little closer, while they talk (Larsen & Smith, 1981).

Physical distance permits emotional distance! Therefore, get a little closer!

*Speaking Personally…*

*How we give advice* is another way to minister. Our recommendations should begin with "I", such as "I would like…" or "I want you to…" or "I would feel better if…"

By using the first person, *"I,"* we show our patients that we have a personal interest in their welfare. We are sharing their burden. They are not alone.

Our time is valuable. Our time with our patient is an investment in them. We give patients our time and our experience to help them. Patients will feel our precious gift of time when we say "I." Our huge personal investment is unselfishly expressed when we use "I."

Let's make some comparisons. Which would you rather hear?

*"You need to get more exercise!"*
vs.
*"I feel strongly that you'll improve when you begin an exercise program. Let's discuss some options."*

*"You're gonna end up diabetic if you don't lose some weight!"*
vs.
*"I am worried about your weight. I believe there are long-term problems if we can't get it down. How can I help?"*

*"Here's your diabetic diet. Any questions?"*
vs.
*"I would like to teach you about good eating habits. Let's begin with looking at your current diet."*

While both pairs of statements make a point, the "I" statements are much more nurturing.

"I" statements prove that our patients are not just a problem to be solved, nor a film to be shot, nor a bed to be changed. Including "I" and "we" shows that we are working *with* them. We are not just technicians fixing a glitch. Including *us* in their healthcare equation will lighten their illness burden and will enhance their self-esteem. Suddenly, they are so important that they are worth our personal interest and our energies.

When we help our patients to make a decision, we can say, "If I were in this situation..." or "If my child were sick, I would...." This reminds patients that we, too, are human and are just like them.

Again, we are letting them know that they are not alone in their quest for good health.

A bonus to partnering with our patients is that they will comply more. When we express our personal interest in their welfare, they now have two people who will be disappointed if they don't follow through. Although non-compliance is a complex issue, we must never underestimate our power as a positive influence. This personal stake in their health is a beautiful way to minister and show compassion.

## Attention: "I'm here for you. Tell me more."

*"When we talk about understanding, surely it takes place
only when the mind listens completely—
The mind being your heart, your nerves, your ears—
when you give your whole attention to it."*
—J. Krishnamurti

Compassion on the intellectual level is demonstrated as attention. When our patients have our attention, they'll know how important they are. They'll know that they are the focus of all our energies. Being the center of our attention will make them feel worthwhile and special.

Patients come to us for our *time*. They may *need* a blood pressure check, a serum creatinine level or an echocardiogram. However, they *want* our time. Without our time, our complex machines are of little value.

In our busy and pressured world, we need to make sure our patients *know* that they have our time. They will only know this by our attention. Remember, they don't see most of the work we do. They don't see us at our continuing education lectures. They don't see us sitting in report. They don't see us reading consultant's notes or digging up lab results. We do a lot of things, for them, that they'll never know about, nor understand.

Therefore, since our face-to-face encounter is such a small part of our work, when we *are* with them, they should know it, without any doubt. The best way to let our patients know that they have our time is by our *attention*. We prove our attention in three main ways: By **active listening**, with **eye contact**, and by saying, **"Excuse me"** whenever we divert our attention.

## Active Listening

If you take nothing else away from this book, please take this: Patients need to talk about themselves, and we need to listen.

Listening is the cornerstone of a healthy relationship. The psychologist Carl Rogers, founder of client-centered therapy, promoted *active listening*. Active listening (as opposed to just sitting there and listening) is a method of gaining a patient's trust and building the therapeutic bond. Dr. Rogers advocates that the caregiver repeat or "reflect back" what has been said by the patient. This shows that they are heard, and understood. Carefully restating what was heard, so the person is certain that we grasp what they said, is very affirming for the patient.

"Reflecting back" has two benefits: It helps clarify what we heard, and it shows the patient that we care enough to want to understand them.

The idea of quality listening is nicely portrayed in Steven Covey's book, *The Seven Habits of Highly Effective People.* Covey's second habit is "Seek first to understand, then be understood." The cornerstone of understanding is *listening* to the other person.

Listening makes our lives easier. When we truly listen to our patients, they will tell us most of what we need to know. They'll tell us the best spot for their IV, which medications work or don't work, and whether or not we are helping. Think of some famous medical errors ... did the surgeon who amputated the wrong limb listen to his patient?

Another huge advantage to developing our listening skills is to get better at "reading between the lines." For example, I once cared for a patient with a very mild cough. He insisted we do an X-ray. The radiology technician used the down-time while the X ray was developing to cultivate a relationship with his patient. The tech listened, and asked a few questions. When they got back, the tech told me that the patient was afraid that he'd aspirated (inhaled) his girl-friend's belly-button ring! The patient never shared that with me, but because our tech was a good listener, we could reassure our patient that there was no foreign body in his lungs. We provided the care that the patient needed because one caregiver listened.

The most important part of listening is allowing patients to speak. One study (Rhoades, et al, 2001) noted that the patient was allowed to talk for a mere 12 seconds before being interrupted. 12 seconds! That just is not enough. We must allow our patients to talk. Everyone has a story to tell. We will be judged as "competent" and "good" only if we let our patients tell their story.

One wise physician taught me, "If you listen to your patients, they will tell you everything you need to know." Dr. William Quinto was an astute diagnostician, and his talents were based on his willingness to listen.

Everyone has a story to tell! If we listen to their story, they will leave us feeling satisfied. All we have to do is pay attention and listen. This was illustrated to me recently on a road trip when I stopped to help a driver whose tow-behind trailer had flipped over. As I got out of my car, I yelled, "Need any help?" He came running up to me, saying, "No…" and he proceeded to tell me in great detail what occurred. I never asked what happened. But he *needed* to tell me, so I listened. Apparently, those few minutes of my attention was all the help that he needed.

*The Eyes Have It*

The easiest way to demonstrate our attention is by eye contact. We can show anyone, even someone across the room, that they have our attention, when we make eye contact.

The eyes are the windows to the soul. Our eyes reveal a great deal to our patients. Have you ever noticed that you can tell if someone is smiling even when they are wearing a surgical mask? The muscles around our mouth that show a smile are under our control (as when we have our picture taken), but the muscles around our eyes reveal a true smile.

Eye contact is very personal. It's the opposite of the dehumanizing medical tests and procedures. It's nice to make eye contact whenever we encounter our patients. And, our patients will think more highly of us when we make quality eye contact (Sherer & Rogers, 1980).

Eye contact means a lot to our patients. It means they have our attention, our interest, and our concern. Eye contact tells our patients how important they are to us. Research on eye contact shows that the duration of eye contact is important, too. Just as no eye contact can reflect our lack of attention, too much eye contact can be intimidating or threatening (Northouse & Northouse, 1998).

Ultimately, you must decide what kind of eye contact is right for you.

Some of us find eye contact too disquieting. If you can't lock eyes with another person, that's okay. Don't be shifty eyed, and look for a second, then turn, then look. Instead, look at their eyebrows, their forehead, or the bridge of their nose. Your patients will feel your attention just the same, and you'll be a more relaxed caregiver.

*Excuses, Excuses*

When we give our time, and our attention, it is important to let our patient know when we have turned our attention elsewhere. There are many *rude* ways to indicate that we are no longer paying attention. We can talk to someone else, make notes, or look away. However, the compassionate way to signal an end of our attention is to say, "Excuse me."

Whenever we are interrupted, or we have to take a call, or we stop our interview to go to a code, we simply put up our index finger and say, "Excuse me." It is helpful to let our patients know when we have diverted our attention. "Excuse me" is the most polite and respectful way of saying, "I am sorry, but I have to divert my attention to something else now. I know you are very important, so forgive me for this interruption." And it's so much shorter! "Excuse me" clarifies any confusion about where our time and attention are focused.

Our time *away* from patients is better tolerated when we show respect for *their* time, by simply saying, "Excuse me." Our patients need to know that *they are too important* for us to multi-task in their presence.

Speaking of multi-tasking, it is helpful to clarify where our attention is focused. Asking permission is one way to do this. For example, while talking with a patient, we sometimes take notes. Before we write, we can say, "Do you mind if I take notes while we talk?" Asking permission to look away proves to our patients how important they are to us. Patients love this! It only takes a second to do, and it really makes people feel special.

## Summary: Compassion
  I. **Empathy**
   a. **Read your patient (Look, listen, feel)**

      b.  Respond to their pain and their emotions

      c.  Use your face to express your feelings

II.  Minister

      a.  Be supportive and comforting

      b.  Touch your patient gently, or get a little closer

      c.  Speak personally, using "I" statements

III. Attend

      a.  Listen actively, reflect back

      b.  Make eye contact

      c.  Excuse yourself when your attention shifts

# *Respect:*
# *Love from Our Spirit*

*"I tell ya, I don't get no respect.... I told my doctor,*
*'When I look in the mirror, I wanna throw up.*
*What's wrong with me?'*
*He said, 'I don't know, but your eyesight's perfect.'"*
—Rodney Dangerfield

Respect is the second pillar of agape. When we love our patients, we respect them. Respect comes from our spirit, our spirit of life. Respect shows that we have reverence for them.

So what is respect? Respect comes from a deep well within us, a well of honor for all living things. We honor all creation as unique, marvelous, and beyond criticism. When we respect another person, we make that person feel *special*.

It's easy to make someone feel special. When they *feel* our respect, our patients will know they are not just a disease, a case, a room number or a call light. Once received, respect is a gift that is cherished.

What about when our patients won't take care of their own health? Do we respect them even though they don't respect themselves? Yes! We don't have to respect bad behaviors or moral transgressions. We don't need to respect their screams of dissatisfaction or their denials of reality. But, as caregivers, we do need to respect them, as individuals. Each and every one of our patients will benefit from feeling our unconditional respect. And, most importantly, they will learn to respect themselves as we model respect for them.

Respect has three primary components. On the interpersonal level, our respect will manifest as **courteousness**. Emotionally, we show our respect through **validation**. On the intellectual level, we show respect via our **honesty**.

### Courtesy: "It's an honor to take care of you."

> "Say 'please' a lot. Say 'thank you' a lot."
> —H. Jackson Brown, Jr.,
> *Life's Little Instruction Book*

Courteousness is the simplest and most direct way of showing respect.

Courtesy is indispensable. It's proof of our respect. Being polite and courteous makes a patient feel worthy, or special, and it promotes their self-esteem. It's a fast, easy and loving way to say, "I respect you."

We show courteous behavior when we are **polite**, when we **dignify** our patients, and when we treat our patients like **guests**.

### Be Polite

We all know *how* to be polite. From our childhood, we are reminded to say please and thank you. Yet, while at work, we sometimes forget … maybe we are busy, or perhaps there are distractions. Nonetheless, politeness will help win the hearts of our patients. Here are three important categories of politeness: Greetings, manners and titles.

**Greetings and Introductions**: A warm greeting, with a handshake and a smile, establishes a caring and respectful tone for the encounter. The few seconds we invest in that warm greeting will yield vast returns. A warm introduction says much more than any words can say. It's easier and more comfortable for our patients to talk when we have given them the respect of a pleasant greeting.

I recall when, as a young graduate student, I fractured my fibula[1] while playing rugby. At the orthopedic surgeon's office, the nurse tucked me into the exam room, and, shortly, the physician walked in, placed the x-rays on the view box, and said, "Here's the fracture." I responded, "Who are you?" He was apologetic, introduced himself, and we had a nice discussion. I think he was just busy, and forgot to say "hello," since he wasn't offended by my question. However, the interaction left a lasting impression on me. To this day, I always introduce myself upon entering a room.

How should we introduce our self? Nicholas Boothman, in *How to Make People Like You in 90 Seconds or Less*, describes the five parts of making a good first impression. He suggests we use open body language (e.g., no crossed arms!), make eye contact, smile, and say "Hi," or whatever our greeting is, and lean forward a little bit. We've already discussed the benefits of eye contact and leaning in a little! Applying these other points may help us even more.

Even when we know the patient, we should still offer a warm greeting. It's *extra* nice to remind them of our name when we leave their room, too. This way, we don't burden our patients with trying to remember our name.

---

[1] Fibula: Smaller bone in the leg. It is found laterally, from knee to ankle.

What about everyone else who is with the patient? Remember, since the "patient" includes visitors, it's nice to greet them, too. If you can't actually shake hands and greet everyone, acknowledge them with eye contact and a nod and smile. We must never forget how important family is. Respect begins with introductions.

**Use good manners**: Polite words offer respect. We should always say, "Please," "Thank you," and "May I." If we must interrupt someone when they speak, we should do so with, "Excuse me," or "I'm sorry, but…" Our patients will tolerate our imperfections when they are softened with our good manners.

It has been said that manners act as a social lubricant. (We all know how important lubricants are in health care!) Manners are another way of reducing friction, of setting people at ease and of underscoring how important our patients are. In fact, manners go beyond smoothing friction; the chivalry and gallantry of good manners allow our patients to feel truly special.

Richard Whately, the philosopher, said, "The very perfection of manners is not to think about yourself." Mr. Whately reminds us that manners are another way to focus on the patient, and not our self. Simply saying "Please," "Thank you," etc. will earn us praise and loyalty, but most important, the effort we take to be polite proves to our patient how important they are.

The opposite of manners is rudeness. Many lawsuits have been filed simply because the caregivers were rude. There are no excuses for rudeness, and the litigation courts prove this. (Virshup, BB et al, 1999, review this topic beautifully. If you don't look at any other reference, look at this one: "Strategic Risk Management: Reducing Malpractice Claims Through More Effective Patient-Doctor Communication," in the *American Journal of Medical Quality*, 1999, Vol. 14, #4.)

**Entitlements:** We should always refer to our patients by the title of Mr. or Ms. These titles, Mr. or Ms., give our patients respect they may get nowhere else. Even if we choose to introduce ourselves by our first name, we should always refer to our patients with a formal title, until they invite us to do otherwise. Never assume familiarity.

This topic is humorously discussed in Oscar London's book, *Kill as Few Patients as Possible*. In the chapter titled, "Don't Call a Rose a Rose; Call Her Mrs. Schwartz," he tells of a patient who became irate, yelling and screaming, when the receptionist called the patient by her first name, Rose. The patient leaves, and vows never to return! Although Mrs. Schwartz's reaction to uninvited familiarity is extreme, the case illustrates our point: patients deserve respect. Unfortunately, most of our patients will not yell and scream. They'll just leave and not come back. Therefore, we should always *give* respect, since it may not be demanded.

I enjoy being called by my title, Doctor. I find it very … grounding. Therefore, I extend the same respect to my patients. However, nowadays there are plenty of doctors who just introduce themselves by their first name, without the title "Doctor." Long gone is the title "Nurse" for practitioners in the field of nursing. However, just because you drop *your* title does not mean you should drop *their* title. We should never assume familiarity and call patients by their first names, unless we are invited to do so.

At the same time, we should be using "Sir" and Ma'am" frequently in our conversations. (Addressing patients with "sir" or "ma'am" shows our humility as well as respect.) We do not need to bark it out like military recruits; it's better to be subtle with this respectfulness in our conversations.

It is particularly rewarding to use these titles with homeless persons, and otherwise disenfranchised patients. This degree of respect is *therapeutic*. It raises their self-esteem, and improves their willingness to work on their own health.

*Dignify Patients!*

The *opposite* of identifying people with respectful titles is to label people as their *medical problem*. We have all used these short-cuts. It is all too common to hear them, such as, "The headache in room two," "The post-op hip in 307," or "The CT[2] guided biopsy later today."

Using a diagnostic label to identify patients is rude, disrespectful and lazy. It disavows our patients as people, dehumanizing them into mere problems. We lose the richness of them as individuals. No patient wants to *be* their disease, and we should never imply that someone is.

(This vile practice is rampant on medical TV shows. I am disappointed by the failure of such programs to set a better example.)

Healthcare is full of other indignities, too. We disrobe people, ask them about their sex lives, and make them wait in uncomfortable positions. While most indignities cannot be eliminated, it is our duty to minimize them, and to keep private things ... private.

Although patient confidentiality is often reviewed by our government regulators and our administrators, it is a topic that cannot be ignored. One of the worst indignities a patient can suffer is to be the subject of gossip. Healthcare is a constant source of juicy gossip ... sexually transmitted diseases, chemical dependency, psychiatric diagnoses, terminal illnesses, just to name a few, are topics that all grab our attention, and are almost irresistible gossip. Don't do it!

Even with supposed anonymity, without names, room numbers or other identifications, others will know to whom we refer. It's not worth it. No one can keep secrets. Please, please never discuss patients.

---

[2] CT: Computerized tomography or computer-enhanced x-rays.

*Host, Versus Staffed*

It's hard for us to remember how very intimidating the hospital, office, clinic, lab or radiology suite can be. Our patients are often lost, confused or frightened. It's helpful if we think of our self as a host or hostess. We don't offer *hors d'oeuvres*; instead, we just conceptualize our patients as visitors in our home. This makes us more aware of their fears and apprehensions when we think of them as anxious visitors, new to our home.

By regarding each patient we see as a guest in our home, it becomes easier to remember the little things that make a difference. For example, we should apologize when there are delays. We should walk patients to the bathroom, or at least offer good directions. We should make patients comfortable, and offer seats to visitors. When there are long delays, it's nice to offer coffee or magazines to visitors and family. Their expressions of appreciation and gratitude are worth the extra effort.

Personally, I will ask permission before any significant physical contact. I often preface *auscultation*[3] with, "I'd like to listen now, if you don't mind." I ask permission before I *palpate*:[4] "I'd like to press on your belly for a minute, if that's okay." I see it as a way of showing my respect for the person's personal boundaries.

While it is true that the patient has already technically given permission for the exam, we need to reduce the *technical* aspects of health care and increase the personal and human aspects. (I have noticed, when I forget to ask, that is when I plop my stethoscope down on a recently healed

---

[3] Auscultation: Listening to the sounds of the body, usually with a stethoscope.

[4] Palpate: To examine by feeling and pressing with fingers and hands.

shingles[5] outbreak or some such tender site, and the patient yelps in distress. I could have prevented this distress by asking permission first, and being told about the sore spot.) The most fundamental aspect of this viewpoint is in regard to nakedness, toileting and modesty. We, in healthcare, see naked people all day long, yet our patients rarely expose themselves to other people. While we cannot let their modesty prevent their care, it is essential to show the utmost of respect when working with self-conscious and modest patients.

Interestingly, each situation needs to be assessed individually. Some patients will appreciate help to the toilet, or help with disrobing, while others are offended by such intrusions. It's nice to ask if they need help. If someone were changing clothes in our home, we'd leave the room, or turn our back, as a show of respect. We should do this at work, too.

Remember, the hospital or clinic is a strange place, full of strange machines and scary noises and weird smells. We must always remember that our patients and their visitors are aliens in an alien world. It's best to offer help *before* they have to ask for it.

**Validate: "Nice job!"**

> *"They may forget what you said.*
> *But they will never forget how you made them feel."*
> —Carl W. Buechner

The best way to show respect on the emotional level is to validate. This simple action will do more to enhance our relationship with other people than almost anything else. Validation is not necessarily agreement; validation is an

---

[5] Shingles: *Herpes zoster* infection, hallmarked by painful blisters, usually in a discrete, unilateral dermatome area.

understanding and recognition of anything our patient has done.

We validate when we allow our patients to **save face**, by **acknowledging** their feelings and actions, and by **recognizing** their unique qualities.

### Face-Saving Measures

This is the most sophisticated and delicate aspect of respect, but when you master this, your patients will love you.

For the most part, our patients act with the best of intentions. As caregivers, we are in a position of authority, a position to have profound influence on our patients. Please, please never condemn, mock or humiliate patients.

To allow someone to save face means to disagree with them, or prove them wrong, in such a fashion that they do not appear stupid. With all our knowledge and technical experience, it is very easy to allow someone else to seem unintelligent. We must *never* do this. Always give someone the benefit of the doubt.

Not allowing someone to save face is very rude and disrespectful. An embarrassed patient will never return, will never trust our institution or us again, and will never be honest with any caregiver again. We should never, ever treat anyone like they are a fool.

This is not to say that we should not *correct* our patients. When they tell us their dangerous behaviors, we must explain the risks they are taking. We let our patients save face through the *style* of our corrections or disagreements.

For example, a woman comes in to see you because of some swelling. She's had severe swelling in her tongue and mouth for two days, since starting on enalapril.[6]

---

[6]Enalapril: Angiotensin converting enzyme inhibitor, blood pressure medication.

She says, "Since there's swelling, I thought a water pill would help, so I took my father's furosemide."[7]

How should you respond? Do you say:

*"Oh, you idiot, do you know what you could do to yourself! Don't you know you should never take someone else's medications! Haven't you ever heard of angioedema?[8] You could lose your airway! Hey, look how this patient treated her angioedema!"*

Or, do you allow her to save face:

*"Hmm, I am impressed that you tried a water pill to make your swelling better, but that's not how I would treat this. Taking someone else's prescriptions can be dangerous. But I am glad you came in, since swelling in your mouth can be a serious problem if it gets worse and you can't breathe."*

It is imperative that you see the difference in these responses! It is good to correct, instruct, advise and teach; in fact, as caregivers, this is perhaps our primary responsibility. However, our *attitude* and *style* of teaching make all the difference. Respect will be felt in the words we choose. Nurturing and loving caregivers will *feel* the embarrassment and shame within someone who is being corrected. We must remember to soften our rebukes accordingly!

One of the best ways to soften any criticism is a feedback sandwich. We used this method when I was a psychologist. A feedback sandwich gives criticism *sandwiched* between two compliments. Our response is: a compliment, then gentle criticism, then a compliment. For example, I once cared for a young woman whose chief complaint was ringing in her ears, and backache. It turned out that she had taken an entire bottle of aspirin over the course of a day to treat her back-

---

[7] Furosemide: Loop diuretic medication.

[8] Angioedema: Recurrent, non-inflammatory swelling, usually mucous membranes; may be associated with use of ACE inhibitor medications.

ache; the tinnitus[9] was a sign of aspirin toxicity. Fortunately, she did not need dialysis. While we hydrated her and alkalinized her blood and urine (using IV sodium bicarbonate), I explained the risks of such high doses of aspirin:

"I am glad you tried to treat your back pain yourself, that shows independence (*the compliment*). However, exceeding the recommended dosage of any medicine is dangerous (*the criticism*). And I am very happy that you knew to come to the ER when you developed more symptoms (*the second compliment*)."

The sandwich (praise for her intention—criticism—praise for coming to ER) prevented her from seeming totally inept or idiotic. And the sandwich reminds us to find, and praise, *any* good behaviors

*Do You Acknowledge?*

An important part of validating is simply acknowledging our patient's words, actions and fears. The opposite of this is ignoring them. Ignoring someone is profoundly disrespectful.

Outside healthcare, people get acknowledged all the time. People get commendations, plaques, praise, money, and recognition of many kinds. Our patients need recognition and acknowledgment, too.

We can acknowledge anything at all. As we discussed earlier, sometimes it's easiest to recognize their fears, worries or anxieties as being real, valid and understandable. By acknowledging their reactions to their problems, we let them know that they are not crazy or neurotic. We reassure our patients. Even if they are worried about something trivial, we must recognize it, and then gently teach why they need not worry.

---

[9] Tinnitus: Noises (e.g., ringing) in the ears.

Acknowledging the *intention* of the other person's efforts, actions and responses, is a powerful way to validate someone. As with the young woman who accidentally overdosed on aspirin, we do not have to *approve* of what she did. But we should recognize her for doing *something*.

For example, suppose you are the paramedic. You are called to the scene of a one-car rollover. The car is on its side. Your patient is out of the vehicle, bloody, limping, and trying to turn his car upright. When he sees you, he says,

"Hey, gimme a hand, it might be dangerous to leave the car sideways!"

How do you respond to him? Do you yell,

"Hey, you idiot! Leave that thing alone, what are you trying to do, crush yourself?!"

Although it is tempting to berate and scold him, it is more important to *acknowledge* his intention. He is trying to be helpful, and prevent someone else from getting hurt. You can acknowledge his intention while you are correcting him.

A validating response could be, "Stop! It's nice of you to be thinking of other people's safety. However, let's not mess with that now. You might hurt yourself even worse."

Our patients will *feel* much better when we acknowledge them.

The conflict resolution literature uses the phrase, "Affirm, even if you do not agree." This phrase is a reminder to allow someone to save face. You might disagree with what they have done or are saying, but you affirm, or respect, their feelings and their right to say what they say. (See the book by Salluzzo, RF et al (eds.) *Emergency Department Management*, which has an excellent chapter by Strauss & Strauss on conflict management.)

Affirming, but not agreeing, is a great way to defuse tension. It's like telling someone with whom we are arguing that we don't agree with them, but we can understand from where they are coming.

It doesn't matter what our patient may have done. Whether it was exercising (but with electrical muscle stimulators), drinking wine for its health benefits (but drinking five bottles), or taking an antibiotic because they felt sick (but a 10-year-old prescription), it is very important to tell our patients that we approve of their *intentions* and *efforts*, even if we disapprove of their specific actions.

We must express an understanding of our patient's perspective, even when we don't agree. This is very validating and very respectful.

In my practice, the most common way I affirm-if-not-agree is with a patient's definition of what constitutes an emergency. For example, while working in the ER one busy Saturday night, a man presented with a lump on the back of his head. This lump was unchanged for about two years, with no pain, drainage or trauma. It seemed to be a benign cyst. I could not resist asking, "Why are you in the ER on a busy Saturday night?"

He explained, "My mother is visiting, and she had noticed my lump. She was getting on my case about it, she wouldn't leave me alone, so I finally gave up and came in here, just to make her happy."

I told him, "Ah, now I understand why you feel this is an emergency. I do not *agree* that it is an emergency, but I see why you feel you suddenly needed care. We all need to keep our mothers happy."

I affirmed. I did not agree.

## Recognizing Their Unique Qualities

We can validate someone many different ways. Everyone is an individual, and recognizing someone's unique qualities is quite validating.

The easiest way to a person's heart is to ask questions about their life. Ask about their children or their grandchildren, ask about their job or ask about their hobbies. When we show a sincere interest in our patients, they feel special.

There are research studies that support this, too. When we chitchat a little with our patients, when we ask about non-medical aspects of our patients' lives, we earn higher patient satisfaction ratings and decrease the likelihood of lawsuits. (See, for example, Roter et al, 1997, for an excellent study analyzing caregiver-patient conversation patterns.)

But remember, our patients will know if we are faking it. They'll know if we are uninterested, or if we ask, but then don't listen to their answers.

Patients should be encouraged to talk about themselves.

Our interest in them, our recognition of their efforts, our amazement at their skills, will *prove* that we see them as special and unique. Further, this is a topic of conversation from which people will never get bored … themselves!

For my own part, I have huge admiration for military veterans. When I have the time, I ask my patients what they did in the service. I remember caring for a gentleman who had been in the Battle of the Bulge in WWII. He could not talk well, from an old stroke. His wife told me about his medals and citations. I shook his hand, and I said, "I am proud to be able to care for such an honored veteran." He began to cry with pride, and his wife later told me that he had not felt that good in many years. On that day, the medical care I provided was trivial compared to the respect and validation I gave him.

## Be Honest and Genuine: "In truth, you can do more for your health than we can!"

*"This above all: to thine own self be true, and it must follow,*
*as the night of the day, thou canst not then be false to any man."*
—William Shakespeare

Honesty is respect on the intellectual level. Honesty and trust bond us with our patients. This bonding is essential for a healthy therapeutic alliance. Before we review honesty, let's briefly talk about its importance.

Honesty and trust are reciprocals, that is, they exist together. In healthcare, both patients and caregivers are dependent on an honest and trusting relationship, in both directions.

Even something simple like explaining the call button to a patient is an example of this honesty and trust. We are honest when we say any call will be answered. We trust that the button will be used appropriately, and we trust that we will be called for important issues, but not called for every petty question. We trust that the patient will use the button in a truly urgent situation. They trust that their call will be answered in a timely manner, and that when we answer, we will be sincerely concerned.

Patients must trust us before they will share their deepest fears and worries with us, and that trust is built from our honesty. However, even when we are in a hurry, honesty must not be forgotten. Therefore, we will discuss honesty with respect to keeping patients **informed**, when we **relinquish control**, and when we **admit mistakes**.

### Keep Them Informed!

Patients want our experience. They need answers. They crave to know what we know. They are starved for information!

However, our patients do not want to *be* us … they just want to know what is going on with them! In the ER, I regularly take care of patients who have no urgent problem, but just want to know the result of a lab test or MRI they had earlier in the week! It's true!

Our patients have no idea what just happened, what is happening, nor what will happen next. For the most part, they do not know why tests are ordered, or how the results will be used. They do not understand the decision-making process. They don't know where the bathroom is. Through no fault of their own, they are clueless!

Everything we do, from dispensing medications to changing linens, from surgery to rehab, is almost never understood. And mostly, that's okay … patients do not need to know about physiology or about how our medical systems function. But they do need to know what's happening, and what they can expect may happen next.

Therefore, keep them informed! Whatever we do, *give a reason*. Whenever a decision has not been reached, explain when they will have the answer. Whatever we do, be it changing their water pitcher to asking for a phone number, we should *give a reason*.

Perhaps the most difficult thing to explain is delays. However, if we just tell our patients what's going to happen, and then estimate how long it will take, they will be grateful. Furthermore, it helps to *overestimate* wait times. This is a technique from business. We should always explain that something takes longer than it usually does. Don't lie to patients; just quote the *maximum* wait time that can be expected.

Patients are so pleased when we tell them what's happening and how long it will take, that it's always worth the few extra seconds. For example, as I leave a room, I usually recap what we've discussed, e.g., "OK, a few X-rays and some lab tests will take about two hours, and then we will talk about the results. Any questions?" Patients love to be kept in the loop.

## Relinquish Control

Everyone loves control. We all know somebody who's a control freak. However, in healthcare, we actually have very little control over our patients. Let them know it!

Remind them of their own control. Let them know that *they* have more control over their health than we do. Have you ever entered a room and have the patient say, "Fix me!" or "Make my wife better!" or "Make my baby stop crying!" Although it is flattering, we should explain that *we* can do no such thing! Instead, we explain that we can offer suggestions which may help.

We need to be honest with them. We can't change *anything* without their cooperation and trust. It helps if we explain *their* role. For example, we can say things like:

*"I can teach you to use a nebulizer[10] to treat your wheezing, but you must use it regularly. And, you must stop smoking."*

*"I can place stitches in your cut, but you must keep it clean and dry and protected."*

*"I will start your IV line, but you must limit your activity, and not pull it out."*

*"I will position this X-ray machine for you, but you must hold still for us to get a good picture."*

*"I can change your linens, but you must ring for help the next time you need to void."*

*"I can teach you back-strengthening exercises, but you must do them every day."*

We need to let them know that they have control over their procedure, their intervention, and their illness. By ex-

---

[10] Nebulizer: Machine to turn liquid medicine, usually bronchodilators, into a mist, so it can be inhaled directly into the lungs, where it is needed.

plicitly stating their role in their treatments, we show that we trust them to participate in those treatments.

There are many ways to let our patients know about *their* responsibilities. It's helpful to choose our words carefully. For example, I avoid saying, "I'm going to admit you to the hospital," or "You need to be admitted." Instead, I empower patients by saying, "I am going to *recommend* that you stay in the hospital," or "I would like to *suggest* that you stay with us for a day or two." See the difference? I give patients *control* over the decision to stay. If it is a matter of life and death, and they want to leave, I explain my rationale in the strongest words.

In general, we should not give *orders* to patients, we should give *suggestions*. We *ask* them to do something; we do not demand it. This helps them be much more vested in their care. Ultimately, they have control over their own health, and it's very respectful to remind them of it.

There's a school of thought that advocates teaching patients about their illness, and then including their input in decisions about their care. It's the field of Informed and Shared Decision Making. It has applications not only for large treatment choices, such as surgery or chemotherapy, but also for simple day-to-day interventions. Asking, and listening to, patients' views are essential to patient satisfaction. (A superb article by Daley, J, [2002] reviews this topic and provides a detailed reference list as well.)

For example, if you were a patient, which of these would you rather hear? "Doc says you need an IV.... Hold still, I'm gonna stick you here!" Versus, "The doctor has suggested you would benefit from some intravenous fluids. Which arm would be better for you to have an IV?" Clearly, the second option invites the patient to participate in their care, and leaves them more vested in that care.

*Admit Mistakes*

It has been said that, "Confession is good for the soul." This may be true, but it's definitely good for decreasing litigation! One reason patients sue is to get caregivers to admit they did something wrong (see, e.g., Moyle, S., 1999).

This is a very delicate topic. All facilities have policies on managing medical errors. Needless to say, those policies take precedence. However, we all make small mistakes now and then, and it's good to admit them and not gloss over them or try to justify those mistakes. For our purposes, let's discuss only small, non-life threatening mistakes. Bigger mistakes you'll share with your supervisor and risk-management department.

Patients do not expect perfection; however, if we do something wrong, they do expect an honest admission of the error. This can be a very difficult aspect of honesty. Admitting when we do something wrong takes courage and trust.

How do we admit a mistake? First, we accept blame. No one wants to hear us whine about how a delay or a lost chart or something is not our fault (even if it's not!) Second, we apologize. (More on apologies in the next chapter.) Then, we ask our patients how they feel. For example, when I omit an important blood test from the initial orders, I say, "It's my fault, and I'm sorry, but we did not draw enough blood for the right test … would you mind if we re-draw?" (Usually, they don't mind; however, if the patient freaks out, I need to re-evaluate the importance of that test.)

The important point is that we admit our error, apologize, and then ask our patient how it impacts them. That is the key. *How do they feel about it?* We want to know, up front, if this mistake is going to mean complaints, poor satisfaction ratings, etc. Often, our *concern* is enough to defuse the problem. Asking how it impacts *them* diverts attention away from us, and our mistake, and back onto the patient, who is the person that needs our attention anyway.

A little bit of humor helps, too. Sometimes I say, "Well, that really instills confidence, doesn't it?" Or some such recognition of how silly we look. However, no big shows, or severe self-deprecating statements, are needed—just a little recognition of the impact our mistake may have had.

The confession of an error or imperfection is so critical to the therapeutic relationship, it should almost never be omitted.

**Summary: Respect**
   I.   **Show courtesy**
        a.  **Always be polite**
            1.  **Greetings**
            2.  **Manners**
            3.  **Titles**
        b.  **Dignify your patients**
        c.  **You are their Host**
  II.   **Validate**
        a.  **Allow your patient to save face!**
        b.  **Do you acknowledge your patients' efforts?**
        c.  **Recognize their uniqueness**
 III.   **Be Honest**
        a.  **Keep your patient informed**
        b.  **Relinquish control**
        c.  **Admit mistakes**

# 6

# *Humility: Love from Our Intellect*

*"Humility is the solid foundation of all the virtues."*
—Confucius

We are all very intelligent, experienced and talented caregivers. We have studied the most complex and useful information on earth. We should be proud of our experience and our wisdom. We should be proud of our greatness!

And yet, arrogance is the first sign of mediocrity. To be truly great, we must be humble, and act with humility. Acting with humility means our focus is on *the other person*. While we are with our patients, *our* agendas, *our* stories, *our* lunch breaks are simply not important. As far as the patient is concerned, we exist for them, to learn more about them, to help them. Period.

Acting with humility is more than merely showing no pride, no pretense, no haughtiness, and no arrogance. For those few seconds or minutes while we are with our patients, we give up ourselves.

Behaving with humility means that all our knowledge, all our experience is directed towards helping the patient.

Just for that brief time we are with them, we are not important. They are. Our needs can wait.

Arrogance or false pride or *hubris* is very damaging. Humility is healing. Humility serves to level the field. Humility reminds our patients that we are no better than they are, even if we do have a little more knowledge or experience than they do.

Humility is best demonstrated in three ways. Intellectually, we **translate** our medical terminology. Emotionally, we **admire** our patients. Interpersonally, we **behave graciously.**

**Translate: "What I mean is..."**

*"Few things are harder to put up with than a good example."*
—Mark Twain

OK, here's a test. Match our word to its closest related acronym.

| | |
|---|---|
| Arrest | DVT |
| Vital | UTI |
| Foley | OD |
| Isotonic | DNR |
| Sick | BP |
| Mets | DIC |
| Clot | MRSA |
| Ewald | VT |
| Hemorrhaging | NS |
| Staph | ICU |
| Code? | 5FU |

How did you do? How do you think your patients would do? This matching game is to illustrate how obtuse and yet subtle our lingo has become. And, we each have many more expressions unique to our institution or office or workplace.

It would be cumbersome, if not impossible, to try to talk to other caregivers without these shortcuts, and their inferences. However, we should never use our special language near our patients, without translating.

Just like any foreign language, *Medical-ese* is a foreign language. Some of us go to school for years to learn our specific dialect in healthcare; others just pick it up from being around. Our various fields of healthcare will, by definition, have some unique nomenclature or jargon. This is very handy. The language of medicine and healthcare gives us shortcuts when we talk about illness and healing. However, we must be careful. Our language can also distance us from our patients, and create an illusion of superiority.

Regardless of how we learned our terminology, we must remember to *translate* what we say, and *translate* how we think, for our patients.

It takes self-awareness to appreciate how ingrained our language really is, *and* how foreign it is to our patients. We should keep it simple. With very few exceptions, we should assume our patients have no accurate understanding of anatomy, physiology, pathology, pharmacology, or any health field.

"Wait a minute!" you might say. "Everyone knows the difference between arteries and veins, or viruses and bacteria!"

This is false. Although most people have heard these medical words, the *significance* of their definitions is a mystery. Defining a word is not the same as knowing if it can kill you or not.

Let's pick on doctors. The book *Surgeon!* by Richard T. Caleel has an excellent example of miscommunication. Here, the surgeon is meeting a new patient for the first time. He asks, "Suppose you tell me what the problem is."

"It's Fireballs of the Eucharist," she rumbled…

"Well, how do they affect you?" I asked, my mind racing, trying to think of something.

"They give me a heavy monthly and a total misery," she said.

That's when it hit me. "Fibroids of the uterus!" I said aloud. Those are muscle tumors of the womb.

She smiled with relief. "That's what I *said!*"

This patient's referring caregiver did not *explain* her medical problem at all. This referring caregiver failed to translate, leaving the patient appearing foolish and ignorant. In reality, it is her caregiver who looks foolish, allowing his patient to have such a bizarre misconception.

Here are a few more examples of mistranslations patients had, because their caregivers failed to translate:

"I was told I might have a bad heart, and I need a *Valium stress test.*"

"My baby has got *chicken pops* ... *look*, they're popping out all over!"

"He was very sick last night, yes sir, he was vomicking up *blood clocks* all night!"

"Thank God my arm is only *fractured*! I thought it was broken!"

"I'm going in to get that *laser* surgery for my gall bladder."

Of course, these patients were referring to Thallium stress test, Chicken pox, blood clots, fractured *is* broken, and laproscopic. We need not be concerned with *vomicking*, a pronunciation colloquialism, not a true misconception. (If you have heard other misconceptions, bastardizations, or poor translations, please, email them to me!)

These examples serve to show the innocence of our patient's misunderstandings, not to mock them. These are just a few of the many half-truths and erroneous notions we can help our patients to avoid. We can best do this via translation.

We translate by talking **in plain English,** using **metaphors**, and by **explaining our reasoning**.

*In Plain English*

No one likes to appear stupid. When we are exposed to a topic that is alien to us, we sort of put together an understanding from the bits and pieces of knowledge that we have. Unfortunately, we are often wrong. However, many of us, especially our patients, feel that it is safer to be wrong than to appear stupid. It's *our* job, as caregivers, to never let our patients misunderstand us.

In general, our patients will not ask for explanations. There are many reasons for this, but a common reason is that they are often embarrassed to admit their ignorance, and ashamed to ask.

In order to fully appreciate this embarrassment, we should think of a time when we were totally confused. For myself, I recall my experiences in the computer repair store. When this teenager starts babbling about SDRAM and kilobytes and downloads and buffer cache and autoexec function and R2D2, my eyes glaze over, and I just sort of nod my head. I leave in a fog, hoping one of my friends can translate for me later.

We don't want our patients to leave with that same sort of partly confused, partly misinformed uncertainty. Therefore, we should use plain English when we explain anything to them.

This is actually a lot trickier than it sounds. Our vernacular is so ingrained, that we often completely forget that a given phrase is actually medical terminology. For example, I once overheard a medical student tell his patient, "OK, when

I get back, I'm going to do an H&P on you." The student then left to get his paperwork, and the wife said, "What did he say?" to which the husband replied, "I think he said he was going to do an Ace, then pee on you ... if he tries that, he's got some explaining to do!" Of course, the student forgot that the letters H and P have no special meaning to patients, and even if he'd said "history and physical," without explaining it, his patient probably would have been almost as confused.

Another good example of this happened when I was in medical school. I had the privilege of caring for an elderly woman who presented with a productive cough. I explained that her chest X-ray showed a mass lesion, and that we would need to get a *tissue* diagnosis. She then reached into her purse, pulled out a Kleenex, and asked hopefully, "Will this do?"

Her innocence made me want to cry. She assumed that her dirty tissue was the type of tissue we needed. *I* had made the mistake. I assumed that she knew "tissue" referred to the stuff from which our bodies are made, and not just Kleenex.

Until we know our patient, we must assume that no medical terms are safe. Or, if we do use medical terms, we must immediately translate what we said. Even the most basic medical terms, such as "extremity," "shock" or "terminal," can be confusing.

When we translate, we cannot allow our patients to appear stupid. We must be very gentle with our translations. For example, we can say, "We think a virus is causing your cold ... remember, viruses are different from bacteria. They live inside cells and most antibiotics have no effect on them." Notice the polite invitation: "Remember." When we say, "remember," we are offering a friendly reminder, not some condescending lecture. It allows the patient to save face. And, in this case, we explain our logic for no antibiotics.

*Metaphorically Speaking*

Another way to teach patients about their specific problem is to translate from medical-ese using metaphors. Sometimes plain English takes too long, or sometimes there is a complex pathophysiological process that does not lend itself to simple translation. Other times, the patient may have experience or expertise in a field that has some parallels to the problem at hand. In these cases, metaphors work well.

Using metaphors (or similes or analogies) means explaining a patient's problem using similarities that the problem has with the rest of the world. This is different from plain English. It allows us to be a little more colorful, and sometimes more succinct.

For example, *atheroschlerotic*[1] artery disease is, unfortunately, common in our society. Remember, atheroschlerosis, and its significance, is quite complex. There's hard plaque and soft plaque and ruptured plaque and thrombosed plaque; there's narrowed arteries and collateral circulation; there's all sorts of complications due to the diminished blood flow. For a patient with atheroschlerotic iliac artery disease (remember, the iliac arteries leave the aorta and go into the thighs, feeding the femoral arteries), we can say, "Your arteries are clogged, like water pipes filled with calcium deposits." The visual image of clogged pipes is much easier to understand than "layers of inflamed cholesterol plaques with a diminished ankle-brachial index."[2] We want to translate their medical problem into a less abstract, more understandable, concept.

---

[1] Atheroschlerotic: Fatty occlusion, narrowing, and lost flexibility or "hardening" of arteries.

[2] Ankle Brachial Index: Ratio of blood pressure in ankle over blood pressure in arm.

The trick is to tailor our metaphors to our audience. For some of our patients, the "calcium filled pipes" metaphor may not be useful. Then, we choose a different metaphor. For a gardener, maybe it's like someone standing on your garden hose. For a police officer, it may be like traffic jamming up a highway. For a mechanic, it may be like debris clogging a car's fuel line. Tailoring a metaphor to fit a patient may take a little more work on our part, but it will pay off later. We read our patients, prescribe the right metaphor for their specific situation, and then we fine-tune our metaphor if it is not working.

We can get excellent practice in using metaphors by explaining things to young children. Sometimes, their experiences in the world are so limited that we are forced to use very simple, concrete ideas to describe those concepts that we take for granted. Try to explain "blood pressure" to a little child. This is a great way to practice translating and metaphors.

## I Think, Therefore, I Explain

Just as our medical language has evolved, so has our thinking. Our decisions are so automatic, we may not even notice them. However, healthcare decision-making is quite complex. And, it is not intuitive. Our patients will never figure us out. Therefore, our thinking needs explaining.

Once we know the plan, we should explain it to our patients. This is as true for a severe illness, as it is for every little thing we do. From a chemotherapy regimen to a blood draw, it's nice to explain *what* is going to happen and *why* it's happening.

Remember, our logic is not obvious to patients. We make inferential leaps, based on one or two words. For example, in the ER, if a patient says, "This is the worst headache of my life," they have triggered, in our minds, the possibility of a *sub-arachnoid hemorrhage*[3] as the cause of the headache. This catapults their complaint from the most common complaint (headache) to one of the most worrisome. Now, we must explain the logic behind ordering multiple tests to our patients.

We mentioned earlier it is respectful to include patients' input when making medical decisions. In order for this to be realistic, they must understand our decision-tree of the options and the possible outcomes.

To do this, we need to explain the *if-then* relationship of our logic. Instead of, "Yes, there is pain medication ordered for you," we can add, "And, *if* you ask for some pain medication, *then* I'll get it for you." By explaining our logic (if you ask, then you will get), the patient is not just waiting around for their pain meds, but instead, knows to ask for them.

Maybe we say, "Let's see if your baby tolerates some Pedialyte," then we also need to say: "*If* she vomits even Pedialyte, *then* she might need an IV infusion." See how it is helpful for the patient to hear the *if-then* progression of our logic?

Our strange logic is the basis for the old joke, "When I was in the hospital, they woke me up to give me a sleeping pill!" But, for us in healthcare, it's not funny. We know the sleeping pill should not be given past about 10 PM, and, come midnight, the patient is going to be complaining they can't sleep!

There are many times where explaining our if-then relationship is helpful. If a patient needs an X-ray, we might say, "Let's get an X-ray ... if your doctor sees a fracture, *then* you will need a cast or splint."

If we tell our patient, "Your blood pressure is low," they might think this is good. After all, isn't *high* blood pressure

---

[3] Sub-arachnoid hemorrhage: Potentially life threatening bleeding, outside the brain, but within the arachnoid covering of the brain, often from trauma or ruptured intracranial aneurysm.

bad? Therefore, we must also say, "*If* you stand up without help, *then* you will probably fall down or pass out." (See how the first part of the statement, "your blood pressure is low," automatically implies, in our minds, the risk of *orthostatic hypotension*[4] and *syncope*?[5] However, this is not the type of logical leap most patients make on their own.)

The knowledge and experience we use to make our recommendations are huge and, often, unconscious. However, by illustrating for our patients *how* we reach our conclusions and advice, we can more effectively include our patients in their care.

### Admiration: "You are quite a person!"

*"Never look down on anybody unless you're helping him up."*
—Jesse Jackson

Humility expressed on the emotional level is admiration. Admiring someone isn't simply *liking* them. Admiration means we look up to them, we are proud of them, and we appreciate their unique qualities or accomplishments.

Nay-sayers among us might say, "Impossible! Only *we* know what really goes on here, they are just ... patients! Patients don't know much of anything ... they are lost without us!"

But of course, the opposite is true: We are lost without our patients.

By admiring our patients, we recognize them as more than a medical problem. Our admiration focuses our attention on the important person: the patient.

---

[4] Orthostatic Hypotension: Sudden drop in blood pressure upon standing up.

[5] Syncope: Fainting, or sudden loss of consciousness.

We admire our patients many ways, including giving **compliments**, showing **enthusiasm**, and simply **trusting them**.

## Give Complimentary Gifts

One of the nicest gifts we can give anyone is a compliment. A compliment does not cost us anything, is easy to prepare, and shows our patients that we have taken the time to recognize them as special.

For example, when someone is in pain, it is nice to recognize their tolerance. We can say, "You must be very strong to tolerate that!" Or, "You are better than I am, I would be crying!" Or, "You could give lessons on how to manage pain!" Our compliments show our admiration for their pain tolerance.

We can compliment our patients for anything, but compliments about their own healthy behaviors are always good. For example, we can compliment them on their recall for their medical history, their blood sugar log, or their initiative to come in to see us.

Most importantly, we can never forget to praise any efforts to stop smoking! Even a small reduction in smoking warrants praise. Even a *plan* to cut back smoking should elicit in us a smile, a handshake, a "Congratulations!" or anything that shows we really noticed what they said.

Further, as we mentioned earlier, praising our patient's healthy behaviors is a *reinforcer* for those behaviors. If we *reinforce* something, it is more likely to occur in the future. And, if we ignore their good behaviors, those good behaviors are less likely to occur again.

Here are some examples of ways to give positive feedback.

Awesome!

Beautiful!

Bravo!

Dynamite!

Excellent try!

Excellent!

Fantastic!

Good for you!

Good!

Great job!

Hot dog!

Hurray!

I'm proud of you!

Looking good!

Magnificent!

Marvelous!

Neat!

Nice job!

Nice work!

Outstanding!

Phenomenal!

Remarkable!

Sensational!

Spectacular!

Super!

Terrific!

Way to go!

Well done!

What a trooper!

Wonderful!

You are a winner!

You're fantastic!

You're incredible!

You're on your way!

You've got it!

We need to use at least one praise phrase *every time* we see our patient.

Compliments are not just nice; they are also a great way to defuse explosive situations. When someone is upset, or angry, or hostile, find a way to compliment them. For example, I once cared for a pregnant woman whose chief complaint was "I almost passed out." The triage nurse noticed that she was in no distress, and her vital signs were normal. The patient had actually just fluttered her eyelids before sitting down. She was asked to wait before I could see her…. The nurses were convinced there was nothing seriously wrong with the patient. When I walked in, with my smile and handshake, I was greeted by her screaming husband. He was irate! "Why did my wife wait so long to be seen!" he shouted. "What kind of hospital is this?!" I let him rant and rave for a few minutes, and when he seemed done,

I turned to the patient and said, "You are very lucky to have such a concerned and caring husband! Many pregnant women have to come here alone." Then, I said to the husband, "Your wife is very lucky to have such a devoted husband. You will make a great father." I complimented him. He calmed down immediately. I was then able to evaluate the patient. By the time they left, he had nothing but nice things to say about our hospital.

We should compliment every patient, every chance we get.

*Be Enthusiastic*

Everyone is important. Every person you meet is very, very important. Every patient's problem, every concern, every appointment, every minute is very, very important. Everything is important to someone. All we need do is recognize that importance. *Enthusiasm* is the easiest way for our patients to know that *they are important*.

When we act with enthusiasm, our patients will know that we truly take them seriously. We must "get into it." Many of the techniques and suggestions we discussed earlier show our enthusiasm: We nod our head, make eye contact, and listen intently. We do these things to show our patient that *they* are our biggest concern.

It does not matter how many other more urgent problems we have to deal with. It does not matter that our last patient and our next patient are dying. What matters is, while we are with *this* patient, we are not distracted, bored, uninterested or unconcerned.

For example, when I interview a patient, I try to look alive. Sometimes I pace the room. I stroke my chin. I think out loud and ask lots of questions. I throw in editorial compliments. I want my patient to know that I am eagerly listening. What they say is very, very important.

The best ways to show our enthusiasm are to **thank** our patients, to **ask some non-healthcare questions** about them, and to let them know that **we are glad to see them.**

**Give thanks.** We should be honored that our patients trust us with their health. Therefore, we should thank them. We can thank them for anything. We can thank them for coming to see us, we can thank them for organizing their medications into a list, and we can thank them for explaining the details of their history for the ten-thousandth time.

We should all express our thanks more often. Radiology techs can thank patients for sitting still, lab techs can thank people for not screaming when their blood is drawn, and aides can thank people for tolerating the sphygmomanometer.[6]

The best thing for which we should be thankful is patience. The glacially slow pace of non-critical health care is very disappointing to many patients. We can thank them for their patience and understanding. It does not matter *why* they are seeking our care, but what does matter is that they know we are grateful for the opportunity to help them.

Showing appreciation for our patients is perhaps one of the easiest ways to bridge any gap between them and us.

As competition in health care increases, we need to be *really* grateful to our patients for their patronage. It's not an honor for a patient to be seen; it's an honor for us to see them. Expressing gratefulness for this honor shows our humble appreciation.

**Ask some non-healthcare questions.** Whenever we have a chance, we should ask about our patient's lives *beside* their illness. Make small talk. However, don't just talk about the weather or current events, talk about *them*.

We can do this while waiting for an elevator, checking a blood sugar or between X-rays. In my practice, my favorite

---

[6] Sphygmomanometer: Blood pressure measurement device.

time for chitchat is when I suture someone's laceration. I ask about their professions, their skateboards, or what they did during WWII. I have taken care of DEA agents, cowboys, bailbondsmen, politicians, drug dealers, engineers, you name it, and I only know this because I *asked* about them.

If we need an excuse to talk to people about themselves, consider it part of their social history.[7] Everything a person has ever done is part of the social history. And, asking social history questions (e.g., Are you married? Have you ever traveled outside the country? What do you do for a living?) is an excellent lead into further questions about that person.

Someone may criticize this view. They may say small talk distracts us from real patient care. They are wrong. Our business is people. The more we know about our patients, the better we can serve them.

In Chapter 5, we mentioned the research paper, "Communication Patterns of Primary Care Physicians," from DL Roter et al (1997). This paper highlights the importance of "psychosocial" chat. Physicians who asked their patients about the impact of their medical problems on their patient's lives received the highest patient satisfaction ratings.

The book, *Improving Patient Satisfaction Now*, by AM Nelson et al (1997), reviews how *successful* caregivers are committed to talking with their patients. These conversations provide important information about, among other things, ways to improve their office!

We can *practice* conversing anywhere, anytime. People love to talk about themselves. When we listen, they will *feel* our admiration for them.

**I am glad you are here!** If we say nothing else to our patients, we should be glad to see them. We are glad to be

---

[7] Social History: Part of a patient's reported Medical History; usually Chief Complaint, History of Present Illness, Past Medical History, *Social History*, Family History, Review of Systems.

taking care of them, glad they chose us for their care, and glad to be with them.

The *reason* for our patient's visit is almost irrelevant. Our opinion about them or their problem is totally irrelevant. All that matters is that we are pleased to be with them.

Many times our patients wish they didn't need to come in. When we tell them we are glad they came in, we agree with their decision. Our patients flatter us by trusting us with their care. We should accept that flattery and thank them for it.

Recently, I was discharging a patient who had had chest pains. This was a healthy, middle-aged man, accompanied by his wife. He had stayed overnight in the ER, got his stress test, and was evaluated by the cardiologists, who cleared him for discharge. While I was sharing with them the routine dismissal instructions, I mentioned, "You did the right thing by coming in. Heart disease is so common in our society, you can't be too careful." A few minutes later, as they were walking out, his wife took me aside and said, "I am so glad you agreed we did the right thing by coming in. I had felt really foolish being here. Thank you." My enthusiasm and agreements with them were very affirming and comforting.

In the ER, this is perhaps the most difficult phrase to say: "I am glad you came in!" However, if our patient is worried that their problem is an emergency, we are worried, too. And if we can relieve that worry, we are glad to help.

*Trust Your Patients*

One of the nicest ways we can show our admiration for a person is to give them our trust. When we trust another person, we create a bond between us. As we discussed in the last chapter, we begin this bond by being honest. We strengthen this bond when we trust our patients. We let them know that we are counting on *them* to continue the therapies or treatments or advice we have shared with them.

In order for a patient to have a successful outcome, and benefit from their interaction with us, we often depend on them, or their family. We depend on them to continue treatments, or to follow up or to let us know if there is a problem. We trust that they will follow through.

For example, after we have cared for someone, we almost always suggest a time for follow-up. We just have to trust our patients that they will make or keep their follow-up appointment. Even if we call them to remind them of the appointment, we cannot be their nanny, following them around, making sure they have transportation, making sure they are awake in time. We have to trust them.

Of course, this level of trust is different for different patients. Children should not be trusted the same as adults. Cognitively impaired patients, demented patients, and some patients with severe mental illnesses cannot be trusted equally. Fortunately, there are services in place for most of these patients. In those cases, we trust the parents, the social worker, or the group home supervisor to follow through.

Just as we discussed in the last chapter (Respect: Be Honest: Relinquish Control), we must trust our patients will do the right things for themselves.

The proud person trusts no one. The proud and cocky amongst us insist that they do everything themselves. The arrogant caregivers believe that no one else can do as good a job as they can. Those caregivers lose the chance to bond with their patient, and lose the opportunity to share their trust.

The humble caregiver will teach the best way to do something, then trust that their patient will do it the best way. Or, they trust that their patient will ask for help.

For example, I once worked with a nurse who would explain every little thing she was doing with her patients. At first, I did not understand why she bothered to teach so much. Gradually, however, it became clear that she was preparing her patients for the time when she would not be there. Inevitably, her patients were always the best at their own glucose checks, or dressing changes, or PICC[8] line care. She could trust them completely because of her efforts each time she was with them.

Once our patients leave our care, we have to trust them to do the right thing for themselves. And, because we took the time to teach them and describe the options, we can be comfortable with our trust in them.

### Be Gracious: "I'd like to suggest that you..."

The word "gracious" captures the essence of humility for healthcare providers, counterbalancing our usual hubris. Being gracious *balances* the relationship.

Being gracious does *not* mean being mousy or being a doormat. Nor does it mean being a sycophant,[9] agreeing with everything the patient says or does. Being gracious allows us to temper our omniscience and pride with a little reality-check. It reminds us that *we* are not all that special, but our patients are.

There are several ways to be gracious. We can **apologize** a lot, we can **ask** (not tell) our patients, we can **sit down,** and we can **smile.**

---

[8] PICC: Peripherally inserted central catheters; Central IV access usually from the arm.

[9] Sycophant: A parasitic, self-serving flatterer. A "yes man."

*Sorry 'bout that*

A proud person does not apologize, nor do they ever admit they were wrong.

A humble caregiver will admit any errors, and apologize a lot.

Apologize. Apologize. Apologize.

We should say, "I'm sorry" frequently. It does not matter if a problem is no fault of our own.

For example, my usual greeting when I first walk into a patient room includes something like, "Hi, I'm Dr. Diering, thanks for your patience, and I am sorry it took so long for me to see you." I say this even if their wait-time is trivial, because I want my patients to know that any imperfection in our service is worth an apology.

We should say, "I'm sorry" whenever our actions are inconvenient, painful, or interrupt our patients in any way. For example, I have worked with wonderful registration clerks. They apologize for having to collect all the usual mundane data, they apologize for *me* when there are delays, and they apologize when they interrupt our interview to let us know visitors are waiting.

There is nothing diminutive in a robust apology. There is nothing self-deprecating in being sorry. There is no implied tort or wrongdoing by acknowledging that we are imperfect, and recognizing that the other person may be disappointed.

I recall, when I was in medical school, a professor actually instructed us, "Never say, 'I'm sorry!'" He felt that any apology was an admission of guilt for wrongdoing, and the apology would show an imperfection in our façade of infallibility. Such arrogance! I could not disagree more! I endorse frequent and sincere apologies.

I've heard that customer service representatives are taught to never say, "I'm sorry." This is good for them, but *we* are direct service providers, and it's okay for us to apologize. If you'd rather not use that phrase, "I'm sorry," that's fine. There are many ways to be apologetic. We can say, "I hate that this is taking so long," or, "Please forgive me for asking this question again," or any other phrase that shows that we care about the way we impact our patients.

In her book, *The Power of Apology*, Beverly Engel provides an excellent explanation of how powerful and beneficial an apology can be, for everyone involved. She states, "Those who are interested in self-improvement will realize that apology has the potential to change their lives, just as practicing gratitude and simplicity has done for so many." Apologizing is an act of self-improvement.

In a perfect world, we may never need to seek another person's forgiveness. However, in the world in which we live, and practice healthcare, an apology humbly builds a healing relationship.

*Ask, Don't Tell*

We should not *insist, order,* nor *demand* that our patients do something. We can *suggest* what they need to do, not insist. We should *recommend* a test or a treatment regimen, not order. We *ask* for a behavior change, we do not demand it.

Gentle words let the patient accept more responsibility for their care. These words also eliminate our role as the all-knowing and all-powerful caregiver. By offering advice, we remind patients of *their* role in their health. *We perform no healing whatsoever.* We merely initiate, or supplement, our patient's own healing abilities.

This is not to say that we should never speak strongly. We aren't wishy-washy when suggesting major life-changes. For example, when we advise an alcoholic about avoiding drinking, we use the strongest possible words. "I want to do everything in my power to discourage you from going to the party. However, if you choose to go, I strongly recommend you bring several AA friends with you. Let's discuss your options."

I have cared for abused women. I recall one woman who was determined to return home, despite having been severely beaten. I explained, "It is your decision to go home. However, I must tell you that I absolutely disagree with that decision. Women who return to a dangerous home have been killed. Or worse. I don't want that to happen to you. Please, reconsider. What can I do to convince you to stay some place safe tonight? I will do everything in my power to discourage you from going back home tonight." I never ordered her, demanded her, or made her feel guilty for her decision. However, I did make my point. She stayed at the shelter that night.

When we make suggestions and recommendations, we empower our patients. When they are later successful or healthy, it's due to choices *they* made, not orders we gave. This is very reinforcing, and gives them the motivation to continue helping themselves.

### Will the Real Caregiver Please Sit Down

Being seated when talking with patients is probably the *piece de resistance* of humble non-verbal behaviors. The importance of sitting cannot be understated. There are several reasons for this.

The most often cited reason for sitting with our patient is the belief that patients' perception of time spent is greater when the interviewer sits down. Since so much of our time is harried and hurried, and since patients often complain that their time with their doctors, nurses, etc. is too brief, sitting is like getting bonus points for the interaction (see, e.g., Schuster, 2000).

Further, it is intimidating to have someone tower over us. People lying in a bed or on a stretcher are vulnerable enough, just by that posture. (The genetic remnants of pack hierarchies are manifested when we lay belly up, thus displaying deference to the alpha male.) Sitting *softens* our position interpersonally. Sitting is less threatening (Purtilo & Haddad, 1996).

Atul Gawande, in *Complications*, discusses how some of the best doctors talk about difficult problems with patients:

"And, often, they don't stand or assume the throne behind the big oak desk, but pull up a chair and sit with her. As one surgical professor told me, when you sit close by, on the same level as your patients, you're no longer the rushed, bossy doctor with no time to talk; patients feel less imposed upon and more inclined to consider that you may both be on the same side of the issue at hand."

Dr. Gawande alludes to the most fundamental reason to sit, which is a social reason. With both the caregiver *and* the patient recumbent or sitting, there is no caste or social order. No one is superior or inferior. No one is poised to attack or run. Sitting infuses the encounter with a casual, relaxed atmosphere. It's nicer.

Of course, we cannot always sit. Sometimes, there are not enough chairs in a room. Sometimes we are just popping in for a second or two. Sometimes we need to be fiddling with our equipment. However, for those intakes and interviews of more than a few seconds, it is very nice for us to sit down with our patient.

Dr. Bernie Siegel feels that being at the same eye-level as our patients is helpful. For children, even sitting may be too high up (Siegel, 2004).

Occasionally, if I need to be in the room with my patients for just a few seconds, to clarify something, I will adjust my posture to them. If their bed is low enough, I will squat down next to them. I briefly assume this position of humility and deference intentionally, to demonstrate my rapt attention. (I also benefit from the increased venous return to my heart!)

*Smile*

The simplest way to show our humility and our focus is a smile. A smile is a quick and simple gift that we can give to almost anyone, almost any time. For our sick, worried and stressed-out patients, a smile can make their day.

We smile because we are happy. We smile at out patients because we are happy to be with them, helping them. Needless to say, we don't smile 100% of the time, laughing like a fool. Being gracious includes being empathic; we may cry with them, at first. However, at some point, a smile is surely helpful.

Volumes and volumes have been written on the effects of smiling. It makes us feel happier, decreases anxiety, and promotes the release of positive hormones (see, e.g., *The Human Face,* 2001, BBC). Smiling is contagious. The smile you give someone else will inspire them to smile, too. By simply smiling, you have helped their health and well-being.

Anyone who does not smile is usually perceived of as a stiff. Nobody likes to be around a stiff. Stiffs are no fun. Unfortunately, some people in the caring professions feel that everything they do is deadly serious, and therefore, they never smile. These stiffs may be technically great, but their patients feel no warmth from them.

Whenever appropriate, I laugh with my patients. I love their jokes, no matter how silly. The opportunity to bond, via smiles and laughter, is a great opportunity, and I seize it when I can. Although *making* jokes is a little tricky, laughing with our patients at situations *they* find amusing is one of the fastest ways to bond with them.

Norman Cousins, in *An Anatomy of an Illness* felt that laughing helped him recover from his severe illness. He rented old comedies and laughed all day long! The movie *Patch Adams* highlights, among other things, how laughing and levity can be very positive, for both patients *and* caregivers. Sharing a smile is very healthy.

In sum, humility is one of the virtues that define love in the healthcare setting. It is easier to act with humility when we remember to translate our medical terminology for patients, when we admire them, and when we can interact with graciousness.

### Summary: Humility

I.  **Translate Medical-ese**
    a.  **Use plain English**
    b.  **Use metaphors, similes, etc.**
    c.  **Explain your thought processes, too**

II.  **Admire your patients**
    a.  **Give compliments frequently**
    b.  **Be enthusiastic and ask about their life**
        1.  **Give thanks**
        2.  **Ask some non-healthcare questions**
        3.  **Be glad to see them**
    c.  **Trust your patients**

III.  **Be Gracious**
    a.  **Apologize a lot**
    b.  **Ask your patients, don't tell them**
    c.  **Sit down whenever you can**
    d.  **Smile**

# *Stories*

$\mathcal{T}$hese stories give a human face to the reminders we have discussed. These scenarios are from the patient's perspective. Although in each case, the care provided is technically acceptable, please pay attention to the *style* of the caregiver's interaction.

After each story, I critique some of the problems with the interaction. There are many more problems with each caregiver than I can criticize. So, I'll just review some of the more salient and serious mistakes. You will notice many more problems than I discuss.

Criticism without correction is not helpful. Therefore, I discuss ways of improving the caregiver-patient relationship. You will probably think of different ways and better ways to improve things. That's good.

Finally, at the end of each scenario, I try to find a pithy or helpful take-home message ... something easy to remember during the hubbub of everyday life. I encourage you to do the same.

# Mr. Rillet and the Stream of Attentiveness

*M*r. Rillet was worried. In all his sixty-six years he had never before had a problem passing urine. Mr. Rillet, a retired plumber, understands the importance of maximum flow pressure in any system. He had always meant to have his prostate checked, but he would rationalize, "Who really wants that exam anyway?"

However, since last night, he has noticed his urine stream getting weaker and weaker, and the feeling of a full bladder increasing more and more. This afternoon, he came to his doctor's office with a massively full bladder, lots of pain and a complete inability to urinate. He has no idea why this has happened. He is anxious and scared. His usual confidence has evaporated.

During the evaluation, he admitted to his doctor that he does have some sinus symptoms, and that he has taken some over-the-counter sinus medicines. Dr. Christie suggested he stop the medicines. Before leaving the room, Dr. Christie said, "And there is really only one treatment for you." She then left the room.

A few minutes later, Nurse Jennie Gallos came in. She was carrying a box wrapped in plastic. As she placed it on a small table, she told Mr. Rillet, "Strip off your trousers and shorts; the doctor says you need a *Foley catheter*."[1] She unceremoniously began opening the package in front of Mr. Rillet.

Mr. Rillet was rather puzzled, but he did as she requested. He had no idea what a *Foley* catheter was; in fact, he had only a vague idea of what a catheter was... "A tube of some type?"

He sat on the edge of the examining table, half naked, nervously watching Nurse Gallos fiddle about with the box, and don the gloves that were in it. He wondered "What's that brown liquid she's splashing on that cotton?"

Then he saw the catheter tube itself. Panic. He gripped the table and quickly estimated the distance to the door, and how long it would take to make a run for it. He had reamed pipes before, and he knew how brutal and forceful one needed to be to get past a blockage, which, he assumed, was his problem.

He gulped. "You're not gonna use that on me, are you?" He desperately asked.

Nurse Gallos frowned and said, "Of course I am, now lay down," and she placed her elbow on his chest to get Mr. Rillet into a supine position. He tried to cover his genitals with his shirtfront as best as he could. She gave him a scolding look as she swept his hands and shirt out of the way with her elbow, keeping her gloved hands in the air. She placed blue paper with a square hole in it over his groin, leaving the penis exposed. He was laying still, a fine tremor over his whole body, sweat running off his face, and his knuckles white from his grip on the bed. He mumbled prayers, begged

---

[1] Foley Catheter: A long, hollow, rubber or latex tube, inserted into the urethra (the tip of the penis in males) to drain the urinary bladder, and allow unimpeded flow and collection of urine.

forgiveness for all his sins, and swore he'd never kick the cat again.

Nurse Gallos was virtually unaware of Mr. Rillet, except, of course, for his penis. She had never been very good at placing catheters, and she certainly had not placed many lately, as a nurse in a family practitioner's office.

As she made preparations, she recalled a teacher from nursing school … Old Miss Avalanche they had called her. She pictured Old Miss Avalanche, hunching over an elderly, comatose man, telling her students, "Grab the penis boldly, with a purpose, and draw it up to the sky. Then, clean the tip like you're polishing your silver, and drive the catheter deep, like you're drilling for oil!"

Now, it was Nurse Gallos's turn. She grabbed Mr. Rillet's penis boldly, digging her nails in a little. He reflexively groaned and shut his eyes tightly. She pulled up to the sky. He groaned again and stopped breathing for a few seconds. She began prepping his penis, as if it had years of tarnish, almost sanding it down with the *Betadine*[2] soaked cotton. Tears rolled from Mr. Rillet's eyes as the Betadine burned the delicate mucosa of his urethra. He was panting now.

Nurse Gallos remained oblivious to the rest of Mr. Rillet, since his penis seemed to be behaving. She lubricated the catheter tip, and raised it over her head, readying herself for the final drive home.

Mr. Rillet peeked. He saw the catheter, but as it was raised, wiggling, backlit by the fluorescent lamps, it looked like a machete! He gritted his teeth as Nurse Gallos swung it down and plunged it deep. She almost expected… a gusher of oil. Instead, the clear tube attached to the catheter filled with yellow urine, and Mr. Rillet sighed a long sigh.

"Are … we … done … yet?" he asked weakly. The relief, the diminished pressure, and the dwindling pain consumed

---

[2] Betadine: Antiseptic solution, related to iodine, used to kill bacteria on skin.

him. He felt better than he had felt in a day. He did not even notice the catheter.

Nurse Gallos, proud of her accomplishment, silently thanked Old Miss Avalanche. Several minutes later, she measured the urine output. "Twelve hundred ccs ... he must have been full," she thought. She fixed the leg bag so he could keep the catheter in place for the next few days, and she left the room to prepare the paperwork.

### Where's the Love?

Even though Dr. Christie is at fault here for not giving Mr. Rillet a complete description of a urinary bladder catheter, and thus the planned therapeutic course, I am more concerned with the behavior of Nurse Gallos. She failed to show love to the patient several times, on several levels.

As is true with most procedures, from starting intravenous lines, or placing Foley catheters, to giving bed baths, and changing sheets, to endoscopy, angioplasty or surgery, performing these strange and unnatural actions for patients is an opportunity to show compassion and respect, with humility. Unfortunately, doing these procedures can also be frightening and alienating to the patient. The risk is that a procedure will be a *lost* opportunity to share love.

**Where's the Compassion?** Did Nurse Gallos behave compassionately? No. Ms. Gallos is actually quite a compassionate nurse ... when she is not placing Foley catheters. She did not empathize with Mr. Rillet, she did not minister to him, nor did she pay much attention to him, as a person.

She offered no comforting or understanding words. She did not ask him how he was feeling, or any other questions, which would have given her a sense of his extreme apprehension. She did not notice the cues he was giving her, like gripping the handrails or shutting his eyes tightly. She completely failed to empathize with Mr. Rillet, and all his confusion and terror. She focused so intently on his penis, she ignored *him*.

Nurse Gallos invaded perhaps *the most* personal part of someone's anatomy, the genitals. We may not be surprised that she didn't say much, since it can be quite difficult to discuss someone's genitalia without schoolyard giggling; perhaps saying nothing is better than silly humor.

However, she could have empathized. She could have placed herself in his position. If she thought about what it would be like to have someone she didn't know, of the opposite sex, jamming tubes into *her*, she may have been more gentle, or more focused on Mr. Rillet. If she had flashed back to her first pelvic exam, and recalled her feelings, she could have empathized with Mr. Rillet, understood him, and comforted him.

Nurse Gallos could have ministered to Mr. Rillet. Before she even opened the catheter kit, she could have put her hand on his shoulder and offered some comforting words. Once she explained the procedure, she could have taught him some deep breathing exercises to help him while she focused on the catheter. Had she been paying careful attention to him, she'd have seen how anxious Mr. Rillet was, and how much he needed her comforting.

**Where's the Respect?** At the least, Nurse Gallos could have shown some respect to Mr. Rillet. Unfortunately, she missed this aspect of showing love, too. She failed to introduce herself, and she failed to treat Mr. Rillet as a guest. She was all business.

She also failed to validate his anxiety. "I know this may make you nervous, but..." would have opened the door to discussing his feelings.

I also was also shocked at her lack of fundamental courtesy when she requested that he disrobe. She forgot to turn her back, leave the room or offer a gown to Mr. Rillet. Sadly, even her choice of words was disrespectful ... she said, "Strip off."

Why would this otherwise good nurse fail to show love for her patient? I feel it is because of the procedure. She was unsure of herself before going into the room. The technical steps involved in placing the catheter distracted her. She lost track of the patient in her quest for optimal catheter placement.

Although perfectly capable of placing a Foley catheter, Nurse Gallos was far too obsessed with the procedure itself. She completely neglected Mr. Rillet. Instead, she provided the Foley catheter exclusively to Mr. Rillet's genitourinary tract, not to him as a person.

**Where's the Humility?** Just because the expression "Foley catheter," and all its associations, is familiar to most of us, we cannot assume that it's familiar to any of our patients. Using this phrase is abuse of medical jargon, and hence shows a lack of humility. If she wanted a warm and trusting relationship with her patient, she should have avoided medical terms. If we must use our obtuse vernacular, we should define the terms with clear details.

Nurse Gallos does not have a huge ego; she is not filled with hubris. She is actually quite a humble and loving nurse. However, when she forgets to explain one technical term, all of her love misses the mark. Her patient is embarrassed at his ignorance, resentful towards her for making him feel stupid, and angry that no explanation accompanied the assault on his urethra.

Appreciate Mr. Rillet's position here. He is not at all instructed about the catheter: he is not told anything about its placement, urethral anatomy, what he may expect to feel, nothing. Nurse Gallos assumed he knows what she knows. She forgot the rule of assumptions: Do not make any assumptions, except that you can assume that the patient knows absolutely nothing about anatomy, physiology, health and medical care.

One technique to discuss genitals is to use strict anatomic terms. By identifying and labeling our patients' anatomy with them, we *teach* them about their prostate, or labia or epididymis or cervix. Also, by objectifying their anatomy, we can discuss it, without the need for nervousness. Further, she could have said, "I am sorry if this is uncomfortable," while she actually placed the catheter.

Nurse Gallos could have made some small talk, and related his urinary-retention problem to his career as a plumber. She could have gotten him to discuss his career, as a distraction. Had she done this, she would have discovered Mr. Rillet's former partner could have helped her with a house she is having built. However, Nurse Gallos lost this chance to listen to her patient, as well as learn from him.

## Do the Right Thing

It's admirable to want to do a good job. In many cases, it is critical to do a great job at the first try, due to the possible complications of any given procedure. However, if we are uncertain, there are several quick and simple things we can do to re-build our own confidence. For example, a brief look in a textbook prior to entering the room can help, or just reviewing the steps of the procedure with a colleague is good, too. Sometimes taking a moment and thinking through the procedure before you enter the room is helpful. (Recalling Old Miss Avalanche is perfect, but Nurse Gallos should have done this *before* she entered the room. That way, all her attention could be on her patient.)

When I need to perform any procedure that I do only occasionally, I like to describe each step of the procedure, and its rationale, to my patient as we go along. This allows me to educate my patient, while I review the details of the procedure aloud, thus teaching and rehearsing simultaneously.

What could we have done differently? Perhaps we would enter the room, ask Mr. Rillet to undress, and offer him a gown. We'd turn our back, even if we were the same sex as Mr. Rillet. Then, we could begin preparations. We might ask if he had ever had a catheter before, and we would explain what one is, how it works, and why it is needed at this time. Remember, patients generally do not know anatomy. A jiffy anatomy lesson while we arrange our kit can be an amazing way to build our patient's trust and confidence in us.

When actually doing this procedure, we would frequently look into the patient's eyes and assess how much reassurance was needed. We would speak softly and soothingly. We would share our patient's anxiety, so we could defuse it. We would let him know that we feel what he feels. We would empathize, and he would know it.

Perhaps it's a busy day. We realize the doctor has dropped the ball on teaching, and we need to do it. We may choose to give Mr. Rillet a quick lesson on genitourinary anatomy with a book, a plastic model, or a poster, and then leave briefly, allowing him to formulate questions. When we return, we glove up and answer his questions, with compassionate and comforting words.

It is also completely reasonable to ask the caregiver who ordered the catheter to go back and explain to Mr. Rillet the plan, procedure and goals. This may be essential if we are uncertain as to the therapeutic plan. Once Mr. Rillet is informed, we can more readily share our compassion and respect for him as a person, not just as a penis and bladder.

**Practice Makes Perfect**

For the next week, at least once a day, try to explain to your patients exactly what you are doing. The tricky part about this is to *tailor* your explanation to your audience. You will not give the same lesson regarding why one needs their blood pressure checked to a four-year-old as you would to an eighty-year-old. How many different ways can you explain about "the top number and the bottom number"? Suppose X-rays are involved ... can you explain about relative densities of bodily tissues to different people?

The ability to speak to someone on his or her level or in his or her own language is one thing that distinguishes the average caregiver from the great caregiver. Some people spend their entire life perfecting this skill, because it has such far-reaching implications. Not only will your patients appreciate the new information you have provided, they will appreciate that you took time to share it, and that you shared it at their level of understanding. You will benefit too, from being forced to learn this information in a more detailed manner, so that you can translate this knowledge for other people.

**Give a Gift**

Give the gift of empathic facial expressions to your patients. Try to match their grimaces, their smiles and their tears. By sharing their face, you will share their heart. You will rapidly learn to feel what they are feeling, and you will expand your emotional and empathic horizons beyond what you thought possible.

CHAPTER

*8*

# *Ms. McLean's Smoldering Concern*

*H*ilda McLean, a thirty-nine-year-old woman, arrived at the clinic with her newborn baby for a routine well-baby check. Amblia McLean is at day of life twenty-eight, but she was born at gestational age thirty-four weeks, so she definitely has not yet reached normal maturity for an infant. She was hospitalized for *meconium*[1] aspiration at birth. Although she was intubated and on the ventilator,[2] it was only for two days. Now, at home, she is off oxygen, on nebulized bronchodilators, and she has an apnea monitor. She has been doing well.

Hilda McLean is six feet tall, slender except for her recently gravid[3] abdomen. She carries herself very confidently, and she has every right to do so. She is director of community development at large government office. She is very attached to her baby.

---

[1] Meconium: Fetal stool. Meconium in the amniotic fluid is a risk factor for lung problems after birth.

[2] Mechanical ventilation, usually positive pressure, requires endotracheal tube to deliver the breaths. Almost always in an intensive care unit.

[3] Gravid: Pregnant.

Amblia is her third child. She is very important to Ms. McLean. You see, Ms. McLean's other two children died. They died, along with her husband, in a car accident, six months ago. She has been with this child continuously since the delivery, and she is not sure she ever wants to be away from her.

Ms. McLean's biggest concern is about herself. She has not been able to stop smoking. She has had "the evil habit," as she refers to it, since she was thirteen. She succeeded in cutting down to about a half a pack a day (at least on good days), but never in stopping. She knows it is a sore point with her pediatrician's nurse, Rainie.

As she sat in the waiting room, she rationalized, "I took my vitamins (even though they must be made in the same factory as *Ipecac*[4]). I gained weight. I have the air purifier, an ionizer, and I go outside to smoke (well, mostly). I wonder what Rainie will say today?"

Rainie has a reputation for being tough with her patient's parents, especially the preemies. However, so far, the nurse and mother have gotten along quite well.

Rainie entered the room, reviewing Amblia's records. She weighed the infant, measured her head and length, and plotted them on the pink graph. She checked temperature, pulse, respirations, breath sounds, and a pulse oximeter[5] reading. "Six ounce weight gain, not too bad ... vitals look good, sats look good..." She handed Amblia back to Ms. McLean.

Rainie was reviewing the patient encounter checklist that Ms. McLean had filled out in the waiting room.

There was a pause, as Ms. McLean, smiling broadly, watched Rainie's face twist. It was as if a distant, ominous

---

[4] Ipecac: A drug to induce vomiting, used in the event of an acute overdose. It is rarely used in any medical setting.

[5] Pulse oximeter: Non-invasive device to measure oxygen saturation of the blood ("sats"), and infer the quality of pulmonary oxygen exchange.

rumble began to echo from afar. The contorted, scowling, reddening face slowly emerged from behind the chart. "Are you still smoking?" she quietly hissed, like steam escaping from crags on Mt. St. Helen's surface. "Are you still smoking?" she rumbled, and the angry lava gurgled and splashed and leapt at the sky. "ARE YOU STILL SMOKING!!!?" Full eruption.

Rainie was in Ms. McLean's face, almost screaming, indignantly. "DO YOU HAVE ANY IDEA WHAT YOU ARE DOING TO YOUR BABY!! THIS IS NO LONGER YOUR CHOICE, YOU HAVE ANOTHER LIFE YOU ARE CHOKING WITH EVERY PUFF! DO YOU WANT TO KILL YOUR BABY?!?" Ms. McLean was frozen in fear and shame, as the scalding words rained down all around her. She hunched over Amblia, trying to protect her from Rainie. Rainie trembled during her eruption, and Ms. McLean could almost see the smoke billowing behind her. The tirade filled the room with white-hot tension and fear.

Then, suddenly, the rage stopped. Rainie looked at Ms. McLean with a hurt, pleading face. "If you can't help your baby, how can we?" After a pause, Rainie scrawled something on the chart and left the room.

Ms. McLean quietly began to sob. Her face was deep red with embarrassment and shame. All her insecurities and fears flooded in at once. In her mind, she remembered the funeral of her husband and children, and the pain was almost unbearable. Her head began to swim as she rocked her baby.

Outside the room, Rainie was saying to the pediatrician, "Okay, I tried the 'irate parent' routine. Now you can try the 'compassionate friend,' and maybe you can get her to stop smoking."

Rainie went on to the next patient.

### Where's the Love?

Although I am sure her transgressions are quite obvious, let us discuss some of the problems with Rainie's approach to Hilda and Amblia McLean.

Rainie fails to show love for her patient in several different ways. The first and most obvious is the anger. Showing anger, or any hostility, towards a patient, is the worst thing to do. Our patients come to us innocent, vulnerable and exposed. No matter how mad we might be, expressing raw anger has no role in the health care environment. Anger is an opposite of love. Even with the best of intentions, the wounds left behind will be long to heal.

**Where's the Compassion?** A recent widow, with a premature infant at home, alone, needs all the compassion, caring, encouragement and love that a caregiver could offer.

Perhaps we can understand not saying "I'm sorry for your recent loss," thus avoiding opening the wound. However, it seems that Rainie just does not care about Ms. McLean's feelings. How can we be sure that Rainie even cares about Amblia? It seems that Rainie sees Ms. McLean's smoking as a challenge to her, a sort of personal affront. Rainie's real goal is to get Ms. McLean to stop smoking. The goal of ensuring a healthy home for Amblia seems to have gotten lost.

Rainie shows no empathy. As a former smoker, Rainie should be very understanding and supportive of Ms. McLean. And, Ms. McLean's pain and suffering from the loss of her family is beyond measure. Saying that smoking could kill Amblia is so callous, so heartless, it's almost unbelievable.

Rainie doesn't even try to minister. She shows no warm touch, no comforting, no personal involvement. Does Rainie care at all?

We should not be surprised if Ms. McLean left the office today saying, "Why bother?" and reverted back to her pack-a-day habit.

**Where's the Respect?** Anger demonstrates a lack of respect. Remember, when we respect a patient, our actions, words, and body language all communicate that respect. Respectfulness can be thought of as a concern for the other individual's personal sense of self.

Even when our anger is focused, there is nothing respectful about that anger. When we express anger, the interaction is about *us*, and our feelings, and not about our patient.

Angry outbursts are selfish. Would you yell at a guest in your home? (Even if you would, don't do it at work!)

We should be very disappointed in Rainie's failure to validate Ms. McLean's efforts to cut back smoking. This is a lost opportunity to praise, to self-disclose, and to bond with her patient.

The anger is not the only disrespect. Rainie was disrespectful when she walked into the room, with her eyes in the chart, and without a warm greeting. There was almost no courtesy here.

Ms. McLean was honest in her admission that she still smokes. Rainie failed to acknowledge the patient's honesty and trust. Ms. McLean did not have to admit she still smokes. However, she trusts this pediatrician's office to handle this personal, embarrassing aspect of Amblia's home life with professionalism and respect. Her trust was shattered.

Was Rainie sincere? It seems that the anger outburst was a ruse, a ploy. I don't think she was *actually* angry. She used her tirade as a tool to get Ms. McLean to stop smoking. This is perhaps the most heinous crime here: Rainie's insincerity. Had Rainie been herself, and stated, with empathy, her fear that Ms. McLean's smoking would cause Amblia illness and developmental delays, she might have achieved her goal. She may have won Ms. McLean's respect and admiration.

Had Rainie shared her personal experiences with quitting smoking, she would have won Ms. McLean's loyalty forever.

**Where's the Humility?** Anger of this type can only come from a patronizing sense of superiority, lacking any humility. Anger shows contempt for the feelings of the patient. The fact that Rainie *intended* to do her patient a service does not count.

While Rainie was ranting, she neglected to even explain *why* smoking in the house is bad for children. Ms. McLean was proud of her ionizer and air filter. Rainie needed to translate some of the research on smoking and *reactive airway disease*[6] into useful information. She did *not* need to erupt.

Rainie showed no admiration for Ms. McLean. As we discussed, she could have complimented Ms. McLean, and thanked her for her efforts to cut back smoking.

Unfortunately, there is nothing gracious about Rainie. If Rainie had seen her role as that of loving caregiver, instead of as The Enforcer, some of her suggestions may have been better received.

### Do the Right Thing

It's not that we are not allowed to be angry. As humans, this will happen sooner or later. However, sharing our feelings in a mature and benevolent manner is the goal. Explosions cause damage... often, damage that cannot be repaired.

If we think of a time in our life when we were yelled at, we will notice the distress it caused us. I recall, when I was an intern, the senior surgery resident ranting and raving because I did not have a specific electrolyte value for a patient. I wanted to die. Further, I was puzzled and hurt, since I was

---

[6] Reactive Airway Disease: Bronchospasm; often a euphemism for asthma or COPD.

being attacked by the person that should have been mentoring and teaching. Though I have forgiven, I will never forget. Anger events leave a huge impact on us, as they do on our patients.

Even though I may have learned a lesson, or even changed my behavior, was I thankful? No. After such an assault, I am left with a myriad of sad, gloomy, shameful feelings. The negative emotions hurt so much, I must tamp them down, hard and fast. This illustrates the painful power that someone's anger can have.

Is this how we want our patients to feel? Never! Further, do we want to be the Pavlovian-conditioned stimulus to elicit their conditioned response of shamefulness or hurt or boomeranged anger, the next time we see them? Never!

Of course, if Amblia and her mother were our patient, we would have behaved very differently. We might walk in the room, chart in one hand, other hand extended in greeting, with a big smile on our face, and our eyes deeply searching, as we warmly burst out:

"Ms. McLean, you look radiant, and Amblia, you are positively beautiful! How are you and the baby doing? Must be great, from the looks of you! Lets see, six ounces, not bad, but, oh, oh dear, you're not still smoking, are you? Oh, how that pains me, Ms. McLean. You, of all people, so smart, so attractive. What can I do to help you? Tell me, anything. Anything I can do, I will."

Or, perhaps we might say:

"Ms. McLean you have no idea how sad I am that you are still smoking. When I was nineteen, I almost died from an asthma attack. I was a smoker then. It hurts me to see you placing yourself, and your child, at risk for more pain. What can I do? Anything I can do to help you quit, I will do."

Remember, being supportive, understanding, compassionate and respectful can help another way: positive reinforcement. Never forget or underestimate the power of your compliments and approvals! While expressing dissatisfaction with a patient's misbehaviors can serve as punishment (a weak tool for behavior change), praise for positive behaviors can serve as a strong reinforcer.

For example, we could have said to Ms. McLean: "Your checklist says you have cut down smoking from one pack to a half-pack a day! That's great! You have cut your risks, **and** your baby's risks, of serious problems! You should be very proud of yourself ... I know it took a lot of work. I will be so happy when you stop completely, which I know you can do!"

**Practice Makes Perfect**

During this next work week, plan to confront a problem patient. Choose a patient whose non-compliant or self-injurious behaviors make you angry.

Then, stop. Ask your self why you feel the way you feel. Plan to share your feelings with your patient. Honestly, directly, but share those feelings in a warm and nurturing fashion.

For example, choose how you would translate "I am angry with you" into a nurturing, helpful revelation to the patient. Perhaps you will say, "I am truly sad that you altered a prescription for 10 Oxycontin tablets into 1000 tablets. You have lost my trust."

Maybe you will say, "At first, I was upset when you said you have not worn your splint for over a month. But in reality, it is very distressing to me that you do not feel as strongly as I do about your health."

Perhaps, you are on the med-surg floor, and an elderly patient has fallen for the third time. As you lift them off the floor, you will say, "I know it is difficult, or even humiliating, to ask for help, but please call for assistance before you try to get up on your own."

## Give a Gift

Give the gift of a smile. Smile whenever you can. Most importantly, smile when you want to be angry. This is one of the nicest gifts you can ever give to anyone.

CHAPTER

*9*

# Ms. Bejanez's Heartfelt Uncertainty

Ms. Bejanez is a forty-six-year-old mother of three. "But I don't feel forty-six!" she would often boast. She eats well, exercises, and has never smoked. She vows she will not end up like her mother, who is an overweight diabetic, or her father, who is a cardiac cripple. She has seen too many of her friends and family end up obese, diabetic, hypertensive, arthritic and prematurely old, and she remains quite active, hoping to prevent such diseases.

Ms. Bejanez usually feels great. Until today. Today she was exercising by riding her stationary bike at home, as she does four or five times a week, when she suddenly felt that something was different. She could actually *feel* her heart beating. Racing. Pounding. Jack hammering. She stopped cycling, and clipped on the earlobe-probe. It recorded her heart rate at 188, which is well above her usual exercising rate of 130 or so.

"Wow," she thought to herself, "is this what a heart attack feels like?

"It can't be.... I don't have any pain ... or can it be?" She knew that, with her family history, it could be. As she rested and recovered, her heart rate did not change much, down to 176 or so. She stopped sweating, and was breathing normally; however, as she sat quietly, she could feel the beats resonate throughout her whole chest. In fact, the pounding of her heart was getting even more noticeable.

She felt like a gong—a gong being shot with a tennis-ball machine-gun. Bump-bump-bump-bump. As she rested, she noticed her hands had a tremor, in perfect time with her gonging heart.

After twenty minutes of this rapid-fire heartbeat, Ms. Bejanez called her doctor. She was asked to come in to the office at once, which she did.

Since it was an emergency visit, Ms. Bejanez was told she'd be seen by the caregiver assigned to overflow, Mr. Josh Moider. She had not seen him before, but she knew him to be one of the PAs in her doctor's internal medicine group.

Mr. Moider has been a Physician's Assistant for six years, and he has enjoyed almost every minute of it. He has a reputation for being an astute diagnostician, and he is respected in the community. The nurse checking in Ms. Bejanez told her, "I doubt you've got anything to worry about ... Josh is great."

In the exam room, Mr. Moider spent a great deal of time evaluating Ms. Bejanez. He performed a thorough medical history and physical examination. He explained to her that he felt her symptoms did not reflect a heart attack. "But," he added, "Your heart *is* beating a little fast. Let us not be remiss. We will need further diagnostic studies. I will order a chest X-ray, an EKG, and several blood tests. And, I would like you to try a little anxiety medicine."

A short while later, just as the nurse was finishing the EKG, Ms. Bejanez's husband arrived. Mr. Bejanez, a store manager, left work early. He was nearly panic stricken. He was more anxious than his wife was. Shortly after he got there, their oldest son arrived. He brought Ms. Bejanez's mother and father. They all came into the room. Ms. Bejanez's mother was silently crying, and her father had a very protective, but anguished, look.

Minutes later, Mr. Moider burst into the room with some flourish. He is waving the EKG and grinning proudly. He blurted out, "I've got it! You've got supra ventricular tachycardia!" Ms. Bejanez's mother almost faints, and Mr. Moider deftly slides a chair under her as she swoons. Ms. Bejanez's son pounds the wall with his fist, and begins sobbing. Her husband leans over Mrs. Bejanez and, with tears in his eyes, he hugs her so deeply she begins to gasp for air. Her father has taken out his rosary beads and has begun murmuring prayers, as he looked heavenwards, his eyes wet with tears.

Mr. Moider is at first puzzled by their reactions, but it does not take him too long to figure out that they assume the diagnosis to be fatal.

"No, no look at this EKG ... it's only SVT, nothing big really, we can take care of it today!" Everyone in the room freezes and glances at the EKG, and then they stare at Mr. Moider, with confused, worried expressions.

"Oh, I am sorry, you have never heard of supra ventricular tachycardia, have you? Well, it's very simple, really ... your heart is racing due to a longitudinal dissociation in your AV node. There is a circuit in there with different conduction and repolarization speeds, such that the signal from the atrio-ventricular node travels in both an anterograde and retrograde fashion nearly simultaneously, to depolarize the heart muscle and, at the same time, reactivate itself, sending the stimulus to beat back down the conduction system, allowing a self-perpetuating electrical event to account for your tachycardia! Piece of cake! I will take you across the tunnel to the hospital Procedures Room for a blast of adenosine, a chemical cardioversion, which is 90% effective in resetting the heart's conduction system, via prolongation of the AV refractory period! Wait right here!"

A moment later, Mr. Moider returned with the permission form. Mr. Bejanez was bear-hugging his wife again, their son was back to pounding the wall and crying, Ms. Bejanez's mother was slumped in the chair with eyes fluttering, and her father was on his fifth Hail Mary. Mr. Moider thought it odd, but concluded this behavior must be... a family thing. Ms. Bejanez awkwardly signed the form while reaching around her husband's massive trunk. Mr. Moider never considered that they did not understand him. He assumed that no one could possibly misunderstand such an eloquent summary of SVT.

When the nurse arrived and moved Ms. Bejanez into a wheelchair for the quick trip to the Procedures Room, her husband painfully squeaked, "What's going to happen to her? Will we see her again?" The nurse replied, "Of course! No big deal ... we'll get her heart back to its normal rate, and she'll be good as new, home in less than an hour. If you'll just wait in the waiting room..."

Instead of overjoyed, the family looked puzzled, and confused.

They held their optimism in check until Ms. Bejanez appeared in the door to the waiting room, looking fit and healthy. Her family cried as they melted with relief and swamped her with love.

### Where's the Love?

What should we think of the care that Ms. Bejanez received? Her SVT was diagnosed and treated, and there were no complications. Mr. Moider even took the time to explain to the family exactly what SVT meant ... or did he?

*Teaching* is perhaps the purest manifestation of love for our patients, but we should qualify this by saying "appropriate teaching" shows love. Regurgitating medical jargon is not love. *Abuse* of our vernacular divides us from our patients. It is demeaning and elitist.

Mr. Moider meant well. He actually did pick up on the family's distress, when he first said "supraventricular tachycardia." He then intended to clarify what he meant, by defining "SVT" for them. However, well-meaning intentions may not be enough to demonstrate love to our patients. Remember, love is an action. Acting with love requires work and effort, on our part.

**Where's the Compassion?** Remember, having compassion means to empathize with, minister to, and attend to our patients. Mr. Moider seems to completely miss his opportunities to show compassion to the Bejanez family.

It is unbelievable that Mr. Moider does not empathize with the anguish of the Bejanez family, either before or after his mini-lecture. Besides his little schpeil, he does not even respond to their grief. A crying patient (or their family) cannot be ignored. Babbling in medical-ese about the benign nature of the medical problem is no balm.

Mr. Moider could have asked the Bejanez family why they were so distressed. If he had let them speak, and listened carefully, or even just attended to their cues accurately, he could have prevented a lot of confusion, anxiety and sadness.

With few exceptions, crying people need to be comforted. Crying, confused and worried people need us to *minister* to them. Even if their tears are completely unnecessary, the act of shedding those tears is a plea for help. For understanding. For compassion. Our *attention* to those tears, and the sadness or confusion behind those tears, is a rich source of love for our patients.

**Where's the Respect?** Mr. Moider was very disrespectful. Although he offered some introductions and greetings, respect is manifested by *courteousness* to everyone in the room, *validating* the patient's fears, and straightforward *honesty*.

Although we regard abusing medical terminology as a lack of humility, it is also rude and discourteous to use words people do not understand. Furthermore, firing complex pathophysiology terms at his innocent targets while ignoring their tears and anxieties is a lost opportunity to allow them all to save face. Mr. Moider permits the Bejanez clan to appear foolish, as their desperate tears and prayers needlessly fill the exam room.

Mr. Moider did have a brief attempt at confusion repair. He actually did notice that they did not know what SVT meant. However, instead of admitting his mistake and mending it, he admitted his mistake, and made a bigger mistake. He definitely should have noticed his lecture was a bigger mistake when the tears did not stop, and he should have admitted it and worked to fix it.

**Where's the Humility?** The biggest problem with Mr. Moider's care of Mrs. Bejanez is his lack of humility. He should have translated more effectively, admired the strength of the Bejanez family, and acted more graciously. It appears that Mr. Moider retreats to the false security of complex medical nomenclature when he is faced with deep emotional concerns.

The emotions which Ms. Bejanez's family displays are very strong and very deep. During his monologue, Mr. Moider grabs the room's attention and steers it back onto himself. Thus the attention is diverted away from the emotions of the desperate family.

Mr. Moider's failures stem from his own self-importance, that is, his lack of humility. When we spout off about things that they do not understand, we are trying to elicit admiration, awe and respect from our patients. If we expect our patients to look up to us, after we dazzle them with incomprehensible medical gibberish, we have failed them twice. Not only have we have failed to successfully teach them about their illness or injury, we have failed to act with humility. Humility serves to redirect our personal spotlight away from us, and onto our patients, who need the light more than we do.

Not only did Mr. Moider fail to translate medical terms into understandable English, Mr. Moider failed to admire Mrs. Bejanez's loving, devoted family. Such caring people deserve praise and recognition for their concerns.

Although Mr. Moider did show some enthusiasm, his enthusiasm was more for Mrs. Bejanez's *problem* than it was for Mrs. Bejanez.

### Do the Right Thing

The two biggest problems with Mr. Moider's care (his failing to teach at an appropriate level and his failure to comfort) are problems, which can easily be treated with a little humility and a little compassion.

Mr. Moider's situation is quite complex. He has his primary patient (Mrs. Bejanez) as well as his patient-family with whom he must work. The family has several generations, and they likely have different levels of medical knowledge. And, he has never met this patient prior to today. These factors conspired against Mr. Moider. Still, these factors are really *opportunities* to show love.

What would we do if we were in Mr. Moider's shoes? How would we teach and comfort the Bejanez family? First, we would have to read our patient's cues and hints, before we could focus on teaching. Crying and distressed people need a little comforting before any teaching. Even just a

"Don't worry ... here is why..." before explaining things may be enough, but we definitely would want to comfort our patients first.

If we are not directly involved with a patient, or if we are on the clerical or housekeeping staff, and one of our patients is crying, it may be enough to touch them lightly and offer reassurances, such as, "You are in good hands," or "Is there anything I can do for you?" or "Let me find someone who can help."

Alternatively, we may just need to console the anguished, and then find someone else to explain events. I have had the blessing of working with very competent nurses and techs. Sometimes, when I just do not *connect* with a patient, I will ask one of my co-workers to help explain their illness or treatment. It's difficult for me to admit that I cannot communicate with each and every one of my patients, but I can't, and I am regularly humbled by this. If I cannot relate to someone, I am not too proud to let someone else do it for me. The goal is not for me to look good, but for my patient to feel better.

If we were in Mr. Moider's place, when it is time to teach or explain, we would craft and customize an explanation that enlightens our audience. We would use simple metaphors. Our goal is to share our knowledge, so as they can make informed decisions. Into this lesson, of course, we would titrate as little medical terminology as possible. We would make sure that we were understood, with a face-saving, "Any questions?"

We would demonstrate our deep interest in them, and our honor at having their trust, by being certain that they understand the problem, and that we understand them. For example, we might discuss SVT as an "electrical short circuit in your heart," or as "your heart is confused about which line is telling it to beat, so it beats several times instead of once," or something. If Mr. Moider had introduced himself to Mr. Bejanez, and asked what he did for work, he could have explained the SVT as "when your delivery boy gets three orders at once and actually does them all!"

Ultimately, the right thing in this context will vary dramatically for different caregivers. If we are the caregiver primarily responsible for this patient, we have the largest burden to teach our patient with love. If we are assisting, we can share our understanding of the pathology, but our job may be to let Mr. Moider know he failed in his attempt at teaching.

Sometimes, when the body of knowledge is too great, or when time is too restricting, we can refer patients to pamphlets or handouts that explain their illness or their procedure. Many offices have a plethora of handouts, which include frequently asked questions for common disorders. We can refer patients to web sites that have more details. Although this may seem like a pass-the-buck technique, people may just need permission to accept those outside sources. The caveat with this, of course, is to be certain that we always ask if we can clarify things later.

When we give our patients our time and our energy, we do so with love and service. We do not really expect anything in return, except perhaps the belief that we did a good job.

Comfort those who need comforting. Teach those who need teaching. We do this with a true interest in their welfare, not our ego. This will show that we can do the right thing.

### Practice Makes Perfect

When you are at work, talking with patients, try to avoid all medical and technical jargon. This is much more difficult than it sounds, since many of these words are now deeply ingrained in our vocabulary. For example, I have caught myself asking my children, "Please pass me that piece of paper, the proximal one." When they give me that innocent, quizzical look, I realize that "proximal" is a technical term, even if it is not a pure medical science term.

When you cannot avoid medical jargon, or when you are concerned about the accuracy of terms, explain in detail what you mean. But, always do this in a way that neither confuses nor shames people. I try to start my explanations with face-saving expressions like, "Now remember..." or, "As I understand this..." so that I do not come off as too smart or demeaning.

Pay attention to your audience! If you are over their head, say things differently. Recall how you felt when *you* were learning the topic.

Never lose an opportunity to demonstrate humility. Our patients want to know that they are in good hands. However, they also want those hands to be soft, warm and gentle.

**Give a Gift**

Give a gift of a metaphor. Metaphors color and enrich our mundane life. The effort to create a metaphor will sharpen our mind and enhance our creativity. Our patients will smile when we make things understood... an understanding just for them. For example:

*This blood pressure cuff is like a hug for your arm.*

*A gallstone is like having a rock in your shoe.*

*A cataract is like having frost on your windows that won't melt.*

*Our computer system is like the Grand Canyon—it's big and beautiful, but takes a long time to get to the bottom of things.*

CHAPTER

# 10

# Mr. Buckram's Twisted X-Rays

*M*r. William Buckram is a trial lawyer. He never misses a chance to make an argument, raise an objection, or explain himself. He'll argue in or out of the courtroom. He is smart, charming, and good looking. He has been arguing his way out of problems since he was a child.

Unfortunately, Mr. Buckram has been on leave from the courtroom for several weeks. He has been working on his recovery from alcoholism. He just finished his twenty-eight-day inpatient program, and he decided to try something new: playing golf sober. Today, as he was getting out of his golf cart at the ninth hole, he fell. His foot stayed in the cart, his hand held fast to his driver, and his right shoulder hit the path first. It hit hard.

The pain exploded in his shoulder. He was almost blinded by the tearing and the burning. He muffled his cry of pain so he would not alarm his partner, who was also his sponsor. But he was worried something was bad wrong. They went to the hospital.

Mr. Buckram tried to pretend that the injury wasn't serious, but the ER physician was concerned about a dislocation. Mr. Buckram winced in pain with any movement of his arm. The doctor ordered X-rays and morphine, but Mr. Buckram refused to accept the pain medication. He did not explain that, as part of his recovery from alcohol addiction, all drugs that could be abused were off limits. He simply said to her, "No narcotics, please." She did not ask him why, and instead offered some ketorolac.[1] He agreed to try a small IM dose.

Rogers, as he prefers to be called, is a radiology technician. He is the best technician in the department. He prides himself on his speed and accuracy. He rarely needs to repeat a film. He is the envy of his peers and the pride of his supervisors in radiology.

Rogers got the order for Mr. Buckram's X-rays.

"Good morning, Bill!" shouted Rogers cheerfully when he arrived to collect Mr. Buckram for his trip to the radiology department. Mr. Buckram was not accustomed to being called "Bill" by people he did not know, and this included Rogers. However, Mr. Buckram was so focused on controlling the pain in his shoulder, he could not quickly formulate an effective retort.

Rogers, in his usual efficient way, skipped unnecessary and time-consuming introductions. As he grabbed Mr. Buckram's good arm, helping him up into the wheelchair, he said, "Looks like your owwee hurts!" Mr. Buckram groaned.

Mr. Buckram was carefully guarding his injured shoulder with his good hand, since the pain was almost intolerable. He'd suffered a few small wounds in Viet Nam, but nothing as severe as this. As he focused on not moving his shoulder, he was beginning to doubt the wisdom of his decision to skip the morphine.

---

[1] Ketorolac: Non-steroidal anti-inflammatory drug for intramuscular (IM) or intravenous (IV) use. It has little or no abuse potential. Trade name is Toradol.

Rogers was quick, but somewhat rough. As they sped through the halls to radiology, he said, "I hope you're enjoying the ride. This is the best buggy in the house!" and "Don't worry about your boo-boo ... after the doc sees these films, she'll get you all fixed up!" Mr. Buckram curled protectively around his right arm, each bump of the ride echoing through his shoulder. Mr. Buckram was quite insulted by this paternalistic chatter, but he was too obsessed with his shoulder to say anything.

Upon arrival to the radiology department, Rogers jolted Mr. Buckram up onto the X-ray table while chanting, "Now, let's see if we can sit nice and still for some pretty pictures." As he brusquely positioned Mr. Buckram for the first of the series of films, he added, "Oh, you are a handsome one, but we can't take pictures of your face today!" Mr. Buckram was getting irate at this demeaning chatter, but he was still too obsessed with his shoulder to organize much of a response to Rogers.

Rogers was pleased with himself, since it only took a few minutes to get all the needed X-ray views, all except for the axillary view. To obtain this view, Mr. Buckram needed to abduct his arm, that is, to lift his elbow up and away from his side. Mr. Buckram said it hurt too much, and he would not do it. So, Rogers then began to abduct Mr. Buckram's arm for him. This caused huge pain, and Mr. Buckram yelped, "Damn it, that hurts!" Rogers didn't miss a beat, responding, "Now, we don't want to make the owwee any worse, but we gotta get just one more pretty picture ... sit nice and still, just like this..." However, as he positioned the arm, Mr. Buckram cried out again and froze. Rogers felt resistance, and tried to wrench his patient's arm into position. A brief battle ensued for control of the arm, and Mr. Buckram, sick with pain and exhaustion, finally begged, with tears in his eyes, "Please, you are hurting me!" Rogers was oblivious, and, aware that his title as The Fastest Tech was at stake with this one last film, forced the arm just a little bit more. As he sized up the film's position, he said, "Now, just be nice and hold on just ... like ... that ... till we get this all finished up, and maybe you will get something special when we get back to that nasty old ER."

Mr. Buckram snapped. He grabbed Rogers' arm with his good hand and, red-faced and fuming, hissed through gritted teeth, "You'll get something special, too, like a pink slip, a lawsuit, and charges for assault if you lay a finger on me again!" Rogers completely ignored the words, removed the patient's hand, and paternalistically replied, "Now, look what you did ... you moved and messed up our pretty picture; now we have to start this one all over again." But as he reached for the injured limb to re-position it, he glanced at Mr. Buckram's face.

Rogers felt the fury.

Rogers sensed he'd be better off not touching Mr. Buckram again.

As he wheeled Mr. Buckram back to the ER, Rogers thought to himself, "I wonder why this ol' bird is so cranky? Oh well, at least I got enough views to prove that there is a dislocation. Let's see ... what's next?" Rogers was oblivious.

### Where's the Love?

What went wrong here? Rogers is the best radiology tech, perhaps the best of the best. The X-rays he obtained revealed the problem. And Mr. Buckram chose to not have any morphine, so isn't it his own fault that he's in pain?

No! When we cause pain, for that moment, it's *our* fault. We know that the patient has given permission to treat them, and that technically gives us permission to cause discomfort. However, regardless of *why* we cause our patient pain, we still must bear some of the responsibility for that pain.

And, yeah, okay, so maybe Rogers is a little demeaning with his endless litany of immature phrases—phrases that serve no purpose, except, perhaps, to avoid meaningful conversations. But, we can excuse Rogers's style since he is so good, can't we?

No, we cannot. Degrading, paternalistic and trite chatter implies complete lack of empathy for our patient. This is not some TV show, where the wisecracking, rule-breaking superstars can get away with anything just because they *are* superstars. These are real patients, who demand our sincere, humble compassion and respect.

**Where's the Compassion?** Was Rogers compassionate? No. Rogers had a job to do, and that job involved a shoulder, not a patient. Rogers was completely focused on obtaining the correct X-ray, and he lost sight of the fact that there was a person—a person in pain—attached to the shoulder. Rogers completely avoided empathy. Not only did he avoid placing himself in his patient's shoes, even when Mr. Buckram begged him to stop, but Rogers ignored Mr. Buckram even when he was confronted vehemently. To say Rogers did not listen is an understatement.

Rogers did not minister. It is almost unbelievable that someone with Rogers' experience could ignore a patient in such pain. Rogers must have worked hard to *avoid* seeing the anguish on his patient's face. He offered no comfort to Mr. Buckram. He was anything but soft and gentle. His grip was harsh and forceful.

It seems that Rogers was oblivious to Mr. Buckram, as a person. Rogers' only interest was in obtaining excellent X-rays. Although this is an admirable goal, Rogers lost sight of his role as caregiver, lost sight of the big picture. Despite his success in obtaining diagnostic X-rays, Rogers failed to *care* for his patient.

**Where's the Respect?** We could say that another of Rogers' faults is a lack of respect. Rogers never introduced himself ("Introductions just waste time," Rogers often says). He failed to address the patient with an appropriate title, such as Mister, and he failed to ask permission to call Mr. Buckram by his first name. Just because he prefers to be called Rogers, he should not assume that anyone else prefers such familiarity. Each offense may seem insignificant, but, in sum, these are quite disrespectful.

How do we feel about the *style* of Rogers' interaction, about his attitude? I personally consider that "talking down" to patients to be one of the most disrespectful ways of communicating. That style dismisses the patient as a valid, intelligent human being, and assumes him or her to be an ignorant child. In fact, even with children, I rarely use this tone.

Rogers showed little interest in his patient. He was completely unable to build any rapport. The rudest thing we can do is to ignore our patient. Even when Mr. Buckram was pleading with him, Rogers' only thought of himself, and his "X-ray tech of the year" title. Mr. Buckram was just so much muscle and bone to be filmed.

**Where's the Humility?** Did Rogers interact with humility? No. Rogers focused on himself. Rogers' only concern was fast X-rays. While his demeaning chatter is rude, it also insulates him from, and elevates him above, his patient.

Talking down to patients is the extreme of avoiding medical jargon, to a negative degree. By talking down to our patient, we dismiss them. It's *easy* for us to assume that anything we do is too complex for our patient to understand, so we'll just gloss over the technicalities of what we are doing with pediatric gibberish.

However, this attitude reinforces the elitist notion of "Us vs. Them" patient care. Ignoring our patients' potential to understand *our* thinking isolates us from our patients, and limits quality interactions with them. Rogers ignores his patient's ability to grasp any of the concepts of radiography.

Rogers had enough time to engage Mr. Buckram in conversation. Rogers never asked Mr. Buckram his profession, nor why Mr. Buckram declined the pain medications, nor how he hurt himself. Quality conversation serves many purposes. Quality conversation is a simple, respectful way to distract our patient from the discomfort of a procedure.

One of the saddest things about Rogers is his lack of graciousness. A technician of his caliber should model the best behavior for his fellow technicians. Rogers never even apologized for the agony he was inflicting.

## Do the Right Thing

What would we have done differently if we were Rogers? Remember, we have a reputation to uphold: We are the most efficient X-ray tech in the department. How can we maintain our reputation, and still show love, when getting Mr. Buckram's X-rays?

Obviously, acknowledging Mr. Buckram's pain and showing some compassion and empathy would initiate a bond between us. Gentle kindness communicates a great deal to our patients. Our patients will be willing to endure more discomfort, if we thank them for tolerating the discomfort we *do* cause them.

How would we show compassion while still shooting quick, quality X-rays? What Rogers is missing, of course, is an empathic recognition of the severe pain which his patient is suffering. We would place our self in the patient's place, and perhaps not even try to get the axillary view. Alternatively, if we had time, we would call down to the ER to ask that pain medications be given to Mr. Buckram. This way, we could obtain the complete shoulder series, without hurting the patient further. It would take more time, but we must remember to put the patient ahead of our selves.

Inevitably, some part of our assessment or treatment will cause, or worsen, pain. Patients understand this, and yet they still benefit from gentle, empathic care. When we are showing love, via compassion, we will try to understand what is bothering the patient. We will approach all contact with a caring gentleness, and we will almost *feel* their pain with them. Ministering to a patient, thus sharing our compassion, is an extraordinary therapy in itself.

Simply showing the patient the respect by using the title "Mister" would go a long way towards ensuring patient satisfaction. We forget that, unlike Mr. Buckram, many of our patients are rarely addressed with a title, such as Mister or Ms. We show honor and respect to a person when we use an appropriate prefix to their name.

Now, some of us might argue that the use of Mr. or Mrs. serves to distance us from our patients. Although this may be true, I feel that the risk of alienation is trivial compared to the benefit of according honor and respect.

Even if it is customary for everyone in your hospital to refer to all patients by their first name, please avoid doing this. It doesn't matter if the patients don't mind. With the exception of children, everyone should be Mr. or Mrs., sir or ma'am. The reasoning is simple: we want to show each and every patient that they are worthy of our respect, and we want to show them that we honor them, by addressing them respectfully.

For Rogers, less patronizing chatter would have helped with this patient. For some patients, that playfulness is distracting, and useful. However, having alternative scripting would be brilliant. Rogers seems to be so focused on the task at hand, he completely forgets to evaluate the patient at whom he is speaking, and adjust the choice of language accordingly. Alternative dialogue would take no extra time at all.

Needless to say, we would show humility while interacting with Mr. Buckram. We would engage the patient and solicit information about them, with a sincere interest. By filling the dead time in this fashion, we not only show humility, we may actually learn something. (Had Rogers done this, he would have discovered that Mr. Buckram would have been very interested in helping Rogers' nephew with his law career!)

### Practice Makes Perfect

Ministering to our patients is a great way to manifest our compassion. Comforting someone in pain is natural; we just need to remember to do it!

Pick one patient with whom you do not get along, or someone who is very lonely, and practice comforting. Get close to them, place a gentle hand on them, and say, "What can I do for you?" Never leave out the "I." Make sure they know you are there for them.

Sometimes comforting involves doing nothing except being present. Lonely patients find great solace in our company. Don't make them create some imaginary problem as an excuse to summon you. Check on them. Call them. Visit them. Be there for them. When we initiate contact, we remind our patient how important they are to us.

### Give a Gift

Give the gift of a respectful title to everyone you meet. Plan to address everyone you may encounter, at work or anywhere, by a title, be it Mr., Mrs., Miss, Dr., Nurse, Counselor, Social Worker, Your Excellency, or whatever. Continue by using sir, and ma'am. I think you will find it humbling for yourself, and elevating for the person with whom you are speaking.

It feels a little awkward at first, but soon everyone will get used to your respect, and will be glad to see you, just so they can hear their title. Your patients, and everyone else, will bask in the warm glow of this respect. At the same time, you will be reminding yourself that this person is worthy of your love.

CHAPTER
# 11

# Ms. Carley's
# Bottom Line

*M*s. Carley is a retired nurse. She graduated from nursing school forty-three years ago. However, she has never done a great deal of clinical nursing, since she worked in the insurance field. She's never had many medical problems, just a little hypertension, and she usually feels good for her sixty-seven years alive.

However, she had noticed a sharp pain in her left lower abdomen several times in the past few weeks. Although the pain was quite severe on two occasions, she toughed it out at home, and it passed. Today, however, was different.

Today she had blood in her bowel movement. Not just streaks, but streams of blood. Dripping blood. Red blood. She thought it must have been gallons. ("Maybe it just looks like a lot, since it's my own," she thought as she stared at the red toilet water.) She called her doctor, a family practitioner. He referred her to the Medical Center immediately, recognizing a potentially life-threatening problem when he hears it.

Ms. Carley had done her nursing school at a hospital that was long since absorbed by the Medical Center, and she feels the facility is huge and intimidating. Nonetheless, she agreed to visit the Medical Center, since she was very anxious about all this bleeding, and she knew that the best of care is available at such a well-staffed facility.

She packed a small bag, and shortly she arrived at the emergency room of the Medical Center. After the requisite paperwork, a third-year medical student saw her while she was in the emergency department. The student proudly announced, "I have to do an H & P on you." Ms. Carley was fairly certain that this meant a history and physical exam. "But," she thought, "it might be a new procedure to control bleeding, too." She was ready for the worst. However, all that happened was that the student performed a complete medical history and physical examination. Ms. Carley did not mind one bit. As a nurse, she was aware of the needs of students, especially at a major training facility like the Medical Center. The student's H & P was very thorough, and, as part of her examination, the student did a rectal exam. The student smeared her blood onto a little green card, and dropped some chemicals on it, thus confirming the "bright red blood per rectum" chief complaint. The student was gentle, and the trauma was minimal.

During the next few hours, Ms. Carley was examined by a fourth-year student, who was a *sub-intern*[1] rotating on the internal medicine gastroenterology service, as well as the gastroenterology service intern, both of whom did thorough, textbook quality evaluations, including rectal examinations. During the course of this extensive data collection, she was told that she would need hospitalization, and probably *endoscopy*,[2] but none of the examiners could really answer any of

---

[1] Sub intern: A senior medical student who acts as a first year resident, that is, intern.

[2] Endoscopy: Use of a flexible, fiberoptic telescope to view the inside of a hollow organ, such as the stomach. A colonscopy uses the endoscope to look inside the large intestine.

her questions. They told her they would need to discuss her case with Dr. Rajan. She had an intravenous line started, blood tests taken, and she was asked to not eat anything. All this seemed reasonable, so far, except perhaps for the repetitious rectal examinations.

Upon admission to the floor, she was examined yet again by the junior resident, and, after what should have been dinnertime, the senior resident examined her, too. Each was very complete in their ability to collect every piece of barely relevant information from her life story, and, of course, each performed yet another rectal examination. In the morning, at 7:15 before rounds, she was seen by the GI fellow, and of course had another in-depth H & P, and another rectal examination, "just to be complete," the fellow said.

By now, Ms. Carley's anus was quite sore. She felt somewhat violated, although she told herself that all students and trainees must learn about this sort of thing somewhere. She felt she was becoming a bit of an expert on rectal exams. She was getting pretty good at estimating how uncomfortable the rectal exam would be, based on how formal the interviewer was during the history taking.

Although not given any reassurances or information about her condition, Ms. Carley was patient, knowing a little about the medical hierarchy. She was expecting the attending physician to provide her with the cause and solution to her bleeding.

At 10:20 AM, hungry and still bleeding, sore in both her rectum and arms (her arms hurt because of the 20 gauge needles used by the *phlebotomist*[3] to collect the q[4] 2-hour hematocrit checks), she heard chatter and noises outside her room. She was hoping she would finally meet the mysterious

---

[3] Phlebotomist: Lab technician who draws blood from patient's veins.

[4] q: Symbol for Latin, *quaque,* every.

Dr. Rajan, and get some answers. Five minutes later, in shuffled the third-year medical student, followed by the fourth-year sub intern, and the intern, the junior resident, the senior resident, and the fellow. All lined up around Ms. Carley's bed, and watched attentively at the door.

A few seconds later, with some flourish, the attending physician entered her room. He was a large man, and he had a full, graying beard. He was serious and severe looking. He assumed the place of honor at the foot of her bed. He announced, "I am Dr. Rajan," and waited silently as he stared at Mrs. Carley. At once, the third-year student began a summary of Ms. Carley's life, and current problems. Once finished, the attending looked at the fourth-year sub intern, who filled in a few gaps, and then up the line, until he reached the fellow. The attending quizzed each one in turn, and humbled each by asking questions just a little too difficult for them to answer. After the haranguing, he declared that he agreed with the plan for endoscopy early this afternoon. He gave a brief didactic lesson on *diverticulitis*,[5] and he then asked who was the next patient to be seen. Just as he was leaving the room, he shot Ms. Carley a patronizing glance and declared, "Don't worry honey, we'll get you all fixed up."

"At least he did not give me a rectal exam," she thought to herself after he left. However, she was confused. She did not really know what just happened. Despite her nursing career, all the medical vernacular and nomenclature they were throwing around was more than she could comprehend. She was hungry, tired and worried. She was still bleeding, still ignorant as to the cause, and still waiting for an explanation as to what might be going on with her gastro-intestinal tract.

---

[5] Diverticulitis: Inflammation of a weak spot in the large intestine, which may cause bleeding and/or pain.

## Where's the Love?

So, how was Ms. Carley's care? Was there any deviation from the standard of care of the community? Technically, there was not. For our purposes, however, the standard of care in the community is a lame standard. It is the *minimum* level of care. It is the *very least* that must be done to assure adequate therapy, and avoid litigation. The standard of care does not require any emotions, or love, or personal involvement, on our part.

Adhering to this standard of care for the Medical Center, Ms. Carley has been evaluated, and a plan is in place. No severe harm has been done. She even reluctantly accepts the multiple rectal exams. Definitive treatment will be forthcoming.

However, we must ask, could Ms. Carley have been cared for with more love? Could her experience have been more comforting and with less mystery? What is wrong with her encounter?

Ultimately, the behavior of the entire gastroenterology service can be seen as the responsibility of Dr. Rajan. We get the feeling that he is a no-nonsense, by-the-book type of physician. We can be sure that under his tutelage, students, residents and fellows learn a great deal about the human gastrointestinal tract. They learn about diseases. However, I doubt that they learn much about the *people* with those diseases. Dr. Rajan sees only the problem, the disease, which needs diagnosis and treatment. He fails to see each patient as a person, an individual who needs his loving care.

**Where's the Compassion?** Was Ms. Carley treated with compassion? No, she was not. Despite her composure and patience, Ms. Carley knows she is suffering from a potentially life-threatening GI bleed. Not one of her caregivers addresses her fears. Her questions are never answered. She is never comforted.

Apparently, no one on the team has been instructed to listen to her *concerns*. They only gather data. Each of her encounters with a caregiver on the GI team appears to be business-like, formal and goal-oriented. No one empathizes with her. No one ministers to her.

Dr. Rajan has set the standards of behavior for his team. He demands complete, accurate, and detailed information for every patient. This is important. However, the information is the *black and white* data. *The manner in which* the information is collected is the *color* of every patient encounter. Patients recall these colors in more detail than they recall the hard data.

What color was Ms. Carley's care? Black and white? Cold gray? Blood red? It certainly was not a soft mauve or a warm peach, now was it? A patient will never remember the black and white part of their care, but they will always remember the color of their care. We must pick the softest, warmest colors to share with our patients.

Another troubling thing about Dr. Rajan was that he almost completely ignores Ms. Carley. Dr. Rajan is the attending physician. Why does he not *attend to* Ms. Carley? He establishes the *tone* for all his underlings on the GI team. It seems that *no one* actually attended to Ms. Carley. No one asked questions about her worries or her concerns. No one asked about her schedule or her family. No one explained adequately what was the plan for this hospitalization. Although her *anus* received a lot of attention, her anxieties did not.

Although we blame Dr. Rajan for the team's lack of compassion, everyone on the team must be accountable for their black and white assessments. Dr. Rajan clearly does not demand rich, colorful, compassionate assessments. He demands only complete assessments. It is up to the other caregivers to fill in some warm colors.

**Where's the Respect?** The caregivers whom Ms. Carley saw lacked respect. Although each caregiver may have behaved appropriately, acting with some manners and decorum, we should look at their actions as a group. The group of caregivers was disrespectful. No patient needs that many history and physical examinations. And, more importantly, patients need to be kept informed about the plan for their care.

Dr. Rajan failed to set limits for his pupils, and, in fact, probably has a reputation for demanding perfection from his trainees. Dr. Rajan is more focused on the completeness of a trainee's evaluation than on how his *patients* ultimately feel. The trainees do as they are told. Respect is not a part of the learning experience on his rotation.

Clearly, Ms. Carley received too many rectal examinations. Where is the dignity in six rectal exams? The rectal exam is an essential part of many evaluations, and critical for some patients. However, it does not need to be done six times in a 24-hour period on one patient. Furthermore, placing one's gloved finger up into the rectum of another person is not a high-tech maneuver that needs extensive practice. No matter how gentle each examiner may be, the collective assault on any patient's anus will take its toll. Amazingly, Ms. Carley acquiesces to all these exams, since she believes in the Medical Center, and in the value of educating trainees.

As further evidence of disrespect, let us not forget Dr. Rajan's parting statement, "Don't worry honey, we'll get you all fixed up." Calling a stranger "honey" is so disrespectful, diminutive and archaic that Dr. Rajan would probably benefit from a reprimand. (I wish Ms. Carley had been an assertiveness instructor for her local NOW chapter!)

**Where's the Humility?** Underlying these failures is Dr. Rajan's complete lack of humility. He fancies himself king of his own little world, and his trainees are his court attendants, while his patients are his serfs. His pomposity is evident from the moment he strides into the room. There is nothing gracious about Dr. Rajan. No apologies or thanks will ever come from him.

No one said, "I am glad you came in today." Although they *implied* it, they did not tell her that she did the right thing by seeking treatment. No one thanked her for choosing the Medical Center.

Even before she met him, Ms. Carley could guess that Dr. Rajan would be full of hubris, since none of his pupils apologized to her for their unwillingness to reveal the plan of care. They were afraid of providing her with too much information, lest it be wrong information, information with which Dr. Rajan would not necessarily agree. Even as they discussed their planned interventions in her room, no one translates for her. Their use of medical jargon and slang is totally alienating, even to a nurse.

Dr. Rajan's GI service is a classic case of treating the disease, not the patient. If he had even a little humility, and established as a focus *the patient*, Ms. Carley, and all his patients, would have believed that Dr. Rajan is working to serve them. As it stands now, Ms. Carley firmly believes that her presence in the Medical Center is primarily for the students' and residents' benefit. She is little more than a living lab specimen, an object upon which they can practice exams. Had she been shown any love, she would have been more likely to respect and trust her caregivers.

Furthermore, he makes no attempt to educate his patient about her presumed disease. He will have one of his minions return to her room later, and give a standardized lecture on diverticulitis. However, that lecture is dry, full of technical jargon, and not at all customized for each patient. It will fail to teach Ms. Carley about her illness, and will serve only to further distance her from her caregivers.

## Do the Right Thing

What would we do? Obviously, if we were Dr. Rajan or the GI fellow, we would organize the GI service so that the H & P (including the rectal exam!) is performed only once or twice, not six times. We would also mandate a senior caregiver to explain all plans to Ms. Carley as soon as they are formulated. Most importantly, we would humbly model respectful and compassionate care for our trainees.

What if we are a peon in the system, one of Dr. Rajan's minions? What can we do? We do not want to be remiss; we do not want to get scolded for skipping any part of the exam, including the rectal exam. Perhaps we would team up with the other examiners on the service and agree that the painful parts of the exam are done only once, while several members of the team are present. If we defer the rectal or pelvic exam, or even the whole history, until several people are present, we can minimize the trauma to the patient.

Suppose we are Ms. Carley's nurse, or aide. We may need to act as a sort of *patient advocate*, and tell the next rectal examiner that the patient has had enough for today. Or, we could ask the examiner to wait till tomorrow, since the patient was complaining about all the repetitious examinations. There are many ways to convince an already over-worked caregiver that they do not need to examine this one patient.

When I was an intern, I had a charge nurse actually prevent me from entering a patient's room! She stood there with her arms folded and said, "Sorry, this patient has had enough for today. She's sleeping." What was I going to do? I stamped my little feet, and I tried to tantrum, but to no avail. The nurse was not budging. So, I let my patient sleep.

Similarly, I have had nurses refuse to place orders for blood draws that could be safely delayed. "Unless it's an emergency, one blood draw a day is all you get." What's an intern to do? I pouted a little, but I realized that my failure to cluster my orders was my fault, and my patient need not suffer more needles because of my disorganization.

It is easy for an intern or other trainee to get too focused on data collection, and lose sight of the individual patient's needs. Thus, others on the health care team can politely redirect the overzealous caregivers to remember that there is a person who is directly affected by every order, every exam and every test.

Whether we are the attending physician or the phlebotomy tech, at some point it is important to ask the patient if they understand what has been happening, or what will be happening, to them. When they stare off with that glassy look, or express curiosity about why tests are ordered, it is important to find someone who can answer their questions. Often the patient does not want to seem uneducated in front of their doctor, so they will ask anyone else, "What is going on here?"

For example, every once in a while, on a busy shift, the radiology tech or lab tech or paramedic student will grab me and say that the patient with whom they are working is not happy, and does not know what is going on. Then, I recall that I ran from the patient's room too quickly, without explaining my thinking, and I humbly returned to the room to apologize, and clarify events for the patient. It is very helpful for *me* to be kept in line by my fellow caregivers.

### Practice Makes Perfect

Before you examine the next patient or take the next order, think about what that patient has been through. In other words, assess your own empathy for that patient. Check your memory for redundancy of tests, or omissions of explanations. Ask yourself, "How would I feel if this were my third rectal exam or fifth blood draw or 37th X-ray of the day?" The recurrent tests may be needed, but please think it through, from the patient's perspective.

Dr. Rajan reminds us to be humble. While you are with your patients, remember to explain *everything* you do. Also, give enthusiastic compliments and thank them for allowing you to help them. Above all, say, "I'm sorry," every chance you get. The more you say, "I'm sorry", the fewer things you will have to be sorry about.

### Give a Gift

Give a gift of a compliment. It does not cost anything. Complimenting someone may do more to help a patient than complex diagnostic and therapeutic interventions. It's a gift that is as fun to give as it is to get.

CHAPTER

## 12

# *Melissa*

*H*er pregnancy had been a nightmare from the beginning. Laurie Vincent had terrible morning sickness. Her nausea and vomiting continued into the afternoon and night so often, that she was diagnosed with *hyperemesis gravidarum,*[1] and needed hospitalization for IV hydration on three separate occasions. To make it worse, her husband, Austin Vincent, had to be away much of the time. His new job allowed them some health insurance, but he had to travel out of town at least ten days a month.

This was their third attempt at having a baby. Laurie Vincent was now twenty-nine. Last year, and three years before that, she had miscarriages. The last miscarriage had been the result of a car accident. And, at age sixteen, she had an abortion.

She was convinced that her difficulties getting and staying pregnant were somehow related to that painful decision made as a cornered teenager so many years ago.

So, with this pregnancy, when she entered her second trimester, Laurie Vincent began to breathe a sigh of relief.

---

[1] Hyperemesis gravidarum: Severe, persistent vomiting in pregnancy, leading to dehydration and poor nutrition, which can be a threat to the fetus.

Relief that maybe she would really have a baby this time, relief that maybe her curse was ended, and that maybe she had suffered enough. Her second trimester went well, until week twenty.

Around week twenty, she began to bleed. Just a little bit, at first. Her obstetrician told her that her cervix was too floppy ("incompetent," he had said), and she needed a *cerclage*[2] to lasso her cervix closed. But all that failed. At twenty-four weeks gestation, Laurie Vincent went into labor.

The IV magnesium slowed her contractions, but ultimately, it was the Vincent's' baby who decided when it was time to be born. At just under twenty-five weeks gestation, the Vincent's had their first baby. It was a girl. They named her Melissa.

The newborn was small, even for her gestational age, at 600 grams. Although the Vincent's had been briefed on the technical risks associated with such a premature infant, they were uncertain if those risks actually applied to their baby.

While Mrs. Vincent recovered from the labor and delivery, Mr. Vincent was allowed to be with Melissa in her new home, the Neonatal Intensive Care Unit (NICU).

The neonatal nurse practitioner, or NNP, in charge was Julie Thayer. Ms. Thayer is quite talented and experienced in caring for premature infants. She rapidly and deftly responded to Melissa's needs. The child was intubated almost immediately, and umbilical lines were placed. Ventilator settings were decided, total parenteral nutrition[3] require-

---

[2] Cerclage: Placement of non-absorbable suture (e.g., silk) around the opening to the cervix, that is, the cervical os, in an effort to prevent premature delivery.

[3] These are life support interventions. Intubation is a tube in the trachea, and ventilate is to have the machine set to give breaths; Umbilical lines are the arterial and venous access tubes. TPN (total parenteral nutrition) is giving nutrition directly into veins.

ments calculated, and monitoring devices set in place. The Neonatal Intensive Care Unit was now Melissa's womb.

While Mr. Vincent went to be with his wife, Julie Thayer worked for sixteen hours straight, trying to balance the technology with the baby. Julie Thayer was a clever and competent NNP. However, that night, Melissa seemed to turn for the worse. A transcranial ultrasound scan revealed a grade 4 intracranial hemorrhage (ICH).[4] The blood leaked into Melissa's left lateral ventricle,[5] and if she survived, she would never be normal.

The Vincents had not seen Melissa for hours, and they had received only vague and incomplete reports.

Finally, Julie Thayer walked out of the NICU to greet the new parents. Mr. and Mrs. Vincent, their eyes begging beyond hope for good news, awaited Julie Thayer's words.

"She has a bleed."

That was all Ms. Thayer said. She turned to walk away. Mr. Vincent touched her arm and pleaded,

"I don't understand ... can't you put a bandage on it, or a tourniquet or something?"

Ms. Thayer did not acknowledge their innocent confusion. She merely looked right through the couple, and droned, "She has an intracranial hemorrhage. She probably won't live. If she does, she'll be total care."

Wearily, she turned to walk away again. This time, Mrs. Vincent, tears rolling down her face, spoke up. "I had an abortion when I was sixteen. Did all these things with Melissa happen because of that?"

Ms. Thayer rolled her head around and absently replied, "You probably shouldn't have done that." She left the room.

---

[4] ICH: Bleeding inside the cranium, or skull, which can be within the brain (intraparenchymal), or on the brain (subarachnoid, subdural or epidural). In neonates, the bleeding is usually intraparenchymal, and devastating.

[5] The ventricles are the spaces in the brain, normally filled with clear cerebrospinal fluid.

## Where's the Love?

I cry each time I read this story. The open, raw pain of the parents is contrasted so sharply by the burned out apathy of the caregiver. Let's look carefully at what went wrong.

From Ms. Thayer's perspective, there aren't many worse feelings than those which surround a lost battle to save someone's life. However, we must never forget that the ill person is only one part of the whole patient. As caregivers, we need to always remember that our responsibilities extend to the family of the ill as well. Sometimes, as in the operating room, or in the ICU, our sick patients only experience the *physical* care that we provide. Our *emotional* and *intellectual* interactions may be solely with the family and visitors.

Julie Thayer is more than competent, and she surely did a good job caring for the child. Despite this, the child suffered an intracranial hemorrhage. Ms. Thayer knows that a bleed of this severity may very well cause Melissa's death. Ms. Thayer is exhausted, and now defeated, and probably depressed. All her work with this small baby was futile.

Ms. Thayer is only human. The sadness of such a loss cannot be ignored nor denied. However, there is no excuse for her behavior. She was a robot. Robotics may have a place in health care, but never when sharing news with a family.

**Where's the Compassion?** How would we describe Ms. Thayer's compassion? Was she able to relate to the Vincent's with compassion from her heart, her mind or her spirit? No. Sadly, Ms. Thayer failed to show any compassion whatsoever for Melissa's parents.

Ms. Thayer failed to demonstrate any empathy for the grieving parents. An important distinction here is that Ms. Thayer *did* empathize. She *felt* the parent's pain. She was devastated by the bad news when she received it, too. She just failed to show it.

As we have discussed earlier, displaying empathy is a quality which distinguishes the mediocre caregiver from the extraordinary caregiver. If Ms. Thayer had just taken one minute to share the pain she felt in her heart, her interaction would have been very different.

Ms. Thayer's lack of compassion also showed up on the physical plane. She failed to touch, hug, or even make significant eye contact with the parents. She may as well have been delivering a pizza.

Ms. Thayer was given an opportunity to redeem herself when Mrs. Vincent asked about her past history of having had an abortion. Ms. Thayer could have listened with compassion, and heard the pain of the sixteen-year-old child, begging for forgiveness. Ms. Thayer could have easily assured the pleading woman, that, the past is past, thereby releasing Mrs. Vincent from her imagined curse. Instead of freeing her, she condemned Mrs. Vincent to years of guilt and depression. Her depression after this loss was so severe, that Mrs. Vincent would later try to kill herself.

**Where's the Respect?** Ms. Thayer was also profoundly disrespectful. She did not offer any warm greetings. A handshake, a validating statement, such as "You must be upset," or "I'm sorry..." would have initiated a bonding, an understanding, which the Vincents so desperately needed.

Although she was honest, Ms. Thayer failed to really show any respect on the emotional level. She showed no genuine interest in the Vincents. The information that the parents had received prior to the labor and delivery was abstract and impersonal. Real honesty demands a regular, enthusiastic updating on the relevant tests and results.

As we mentioned earlier, Julie Thayer was told a secret. Mrs. Vincent did not need to mention her abortion. Ms. Thayer was offered deeply personal and painful information that Mrs. Vincent did not need to share. Such a secret is fragile. It is as fragile as a tiny glass amulet. An amulet full of poison. This amulet was entrusted to Ms. Thayer. Ms. Thayer dismissively crushed it, grinding the shards of the secret into Mrs. Vincent's heart.

No matter how tired or how depressed a caregiver may be, there is never an excuse to shatter trust. We do not pass judgment.

**Where's the Humility?** Ms. Thayer's apathy was also evident in her lack of humility. As a wall between her and the parents, Ms. Thayer used medical slang ("a bleed"), and then defined this slang with medical jargon ("intracranial hemorrhage"). She then used medical slang again ("total care"), and did not even attempt to define this phrase.

Furthermore, she failed to show any admiration, since she did not compliment or praise the desperate family for their patience through this ordeal.

We can suspect Ms. Thayer is protecting herself from the pain of Melissa's care, but this cannot be an excuse for such behavior. We should want to scream at Ms. Thayer, shake her and point to the family, saying, "Look what you are doing to them!"

## Do the Right Thing

This caregiver is out of control. Even at our most exhausted and depleted moments, *we* would never be so callous ... or would we?

What is the right thing to do?

For those of us who express ourselves well, we would cry. Our love would manifest in our tears. We would hold the parents, and sob with them over the inevitable loss of this, their so desperately desired infant. We would show that we feel their pain.

Even if exhausted, we would try to explain everything that we did, in detail, but in everyday language. If the parents understand what we have done, if they know that we did everything we could, this helps them to achieve closure, to accept their child's likely death.

Acknowledging our pain, as well as someone else's pain, even for a few minutes, is very difficult. It really hurts. However, although it hurts, as we cry or grieve with our patient's families, the brief union serves to make each of us better for the experience. It may give *us* closure, too.

We would never condemn Mrs. Vincent for her past abortion. Even if we are a devout right-to-life advocate, or if we felt that the abortion may have left uterine scars, we would know that there is a time and a place for reproductive counseling. The NICU waiting room is not it.

Perhaps we are not able to express our self well. If we understand our own emotional ability, crying might seem faked. Regardless of how we express our feelings, we would still express sadness. We would sit down with the parents, hold hands or touch them gently on their shoulder or knee. We would make compassionate eye contact, and explain, in understandable terms, all that has transpired. We would explain the significance of the hemorrhage. We would show some sadness, and say "I'm sorry" as we describe the possible outcomes. We would praise them for being patient and being strong. We would thank them for their trust in us.

Knowing our own limits, perhaps we would need to explain that we are tired, and it is late, and that we will answer their questions later.

Of course, if we are bad at reading other people's pain, empathizing, and expressing our feelings, we may need to bring someone along with us. Melissa's nurse, the neonatologist, the chaplain, or anyone who is adept at offering moral support could help us break the bad news and assist in comforting the family. This strategy is helpful especially when we have had such a bad day we could never give a quality, caring explanation.

However, as a caregiver who really cares, we will want to share severe news ourself. We will never dump the responsibility onto someone else.

(When I was an emergency medicine resident in training, I had the nickname of "Father Scott," because my fellow physicians noticed the empathic manner in which I shared bad news. And, we had a lot of bad news to share. Usually, I would put my hand on the surviving family member while they cried, and I would say, "I'm so sorry, I'm so sorry" over and over. While this came naturally to me, my peers were curious. Sometimes, these other physicians would enlist me to help them share bad news, even if I was not involved with the deceased patient's care. I would not do someone else's work; when one of my co-workers felt they needed help in telling the family about the death, I would go along for support. I was supporting my fellow caregivers, and I was glad to model my style of comforting as I helped console the anguished family. I wanted the family to know we cared, and I respected my peers' awareness of their limits.)

Of course, the opposite situation may be true. If we feel we are much better at compassion and consoling than the primary caregiver, we will need to go with them to break bad news. Then, we can remain behind after the socially unskilled caregiver has left, and we can touch, hug, and cry with the grieving family.

When I trained in neurosurgery, I witnessed some shockingly inhumane ways of giving bad news. Whenever this happened, I would stay behind after the attending neurosurgeon left the scene. I would translate for, and comfort, the stunned family. Similarly, I would often volunteer to broach the subject of organ donation to families.

As loving caregivers, we must evaluate our role in the health care team. On some days, we may be the worst caregiver for delivering news, terrible at teaching or too distracted to empathize. On these days, it may be best to work with someone else to share and instruct. At other times, with different team members or on better days, we may need to take it upon our own to do more direct patient caring and teaching.

Regardless of how we assess our role in the care team, we should always imagine our self as the patient, and think what is best for them. Whatever we do, we do for our patient.

**Practice Makes Perfect**

I hope you do not find this homework too touchy-feely, because it can have life-changing ramifications.

This week, try to imagine how someone else is feeling. To do this, pick someone you do not know that well, but someone with whom you have a relationship... perhaps a fellow caregiver. Take a few minutes. Imagine their motivations, their goals, and their greatest fears. Imagine their daily routine before you saw them. Include as much detail as you can conjure up, and the more imagination you use, the better. You can do this while driving to work or while taking a break. Picture their living arrangements, what they had for breakfast, and their trip into work. Just for a few minutes, carry this person's life within you, and see if you are better able to understand their behavior.

Once you have done this exercise a few times, do it again, except choose a person with whom you do not get along, someone you do not like. Imagine what their life must be like, and how they perceive the world. Avoid jealousy and malice. I want you to fill in the details of their life, using your imagination, not hearsay or second-hand reports.

Finally, after you are able to see the pain and anguish that this person lives with, imagine yourself telling them you are sorry. Imagine consoling and comforting this person whom you dislike. Picture this person happy and at ease, grateful for your kindness.

Once you practice this exercise over and over, you will be amazed at the improvement in your ability to instantly empathize.

## Give a Gift

Give the gift of a warm touch. Make sure your touch is above and beyond any contact necessary for your job. Soft, sincere physical contact with another person is an excellent way to initiate empathy, and it communicates many nice things at once.

CHAPTER

## *13*

# *Ms. Griffin's Show*

*M*s. Griffin was trying to enjoy the ride, but decided there was nothing enjoyable about being tightly strapped to a stretcher, bouncing along in the back of an ambulance. Until last week, she had never ridden in an ambulance, and here is her second ride in ten days.

Ms. Griffin is seventy-six. She is being transported from the hospital to a "facility for intensive physical therapy." She just had surgery on her ankle, and she recognized the wisdom of a few weeks at a "convalescent center" for physical therapy.

Yes, a "convalescent center." She refused to think of it as a nursing home. However, a nursing home is exactly what the facility is to most of its residents.

"For *me*," thought Ms. Griffin, "this will be a little vacation. A working vacation, so I can learn to walk carefully with crutches and a walker."

Ms. Griffin is a retired high school English teacher. She used to coach the Debate and Forensic Club as well, and she loves discussion and verbal jousting. Since her husband died six years ago, she has kept her skills up during her weekly bridge club, as well as on the internet, via chat rooms and web columns.

She had even convinced her orthopedic surgeon to let her go home, with home health visits. However, she agreed to the convalescent center (*not* nursing home) only *after* she won the debate with the doctor. She was proud of her argument, most of which was extemporaneous, and her victory, yet she understood the need for intensive physical therapy.

When the ambulance pulled up in front of Cottonwood Acres, the paramedics whipped open the doors and un-latched the stretcher from the floor locks. "I hope I am not too heavy for you boys ... what is the most weight you have ever had to carry on one of these gurneys?" Ms. Griffin asked, trying to make conversation. There was no reply. One medic said, "Where we goin'?" to which the other replied, "One-seventeen, don't you ever look at the paperwork?" They unceremoniously plopped the wheels down and began to roll inside.

Once inside, the receptionist came around to the counter, shuffling some papers. Ms. Griffin tried to look into her unfocused eyes, and said, "A lovely place you have, how many people stay here at one time?" The receptionist stared at her papers, and asked the paramedic, "Is this the one from Jewish?" To which the medic responded, "Yeah, she's a walkie-talkie, too."

"Great. One-seventeen, I'll bring the paper work in later." Ms. Griffin puzzled over her newfound invisibility, wondering how she was now a "walkie-talkie" as they rolled down the hall.

Once in her room, she considered trying to converse with the medics again, but decided against it. As they rolled up their straps, the nurse came into the room. The nurse stuck out her hand to the paramedics saying, "We haven't gotten any orders yet, let's see whatcha got there." Ms.

Griffin spoke up, "I have a *bi-malleolar fracture*,[1] which Dr. Gomez took care of with an O-R-I-F, I believe."

As the nurse glanced at the transfer summary, she said to the medics, "Looks like a busted ankle, better than that guy on TV last night."

"Oh yeah, did you see that? Nasty stuff," said the more communicative medic.

The nurse's aide was entering the room as he said it, and she asked, "What's nasty, not our new resident?"

"No, this guy on TV last night, had his foot surgically re-attached after it was chopped off," the paramedic said, as he gestured the amputation with his hands.

The aide began to take Ms. Griffin's blood pressure, but was talking to the medic, "Yeah, I seen that, his girlfriend chopped his foot off with an ax, didn't she, and he had to hobble to the fridge, carrying his foot, just to get ice, so his foot wouldn't rot, the whole time he was bleeding all over!"

In came the housekeeper, shrieking, "What blood all over? I just cleaned this room!" she said, as she snooped around, looking for a mess.

"No, no, on TV last night," the nurse filled in the house-keeper, "this guy had his foot chopped off!"

"Oh with the ax, right, I saw that, but you know what really happened? Did you see the coming attractions for next week's show? We find out that there was this big dog that bit him, a Rottweiller or something..."

Just then, the security guard walked in, sternly asking "What dog? No dogs in this facility! It's got to go."

But the housekeeper described the show, and the security guard added, to everyone's amazement, "Yeah, it's a real

---

[1] Bi-malleolar fracture: An unstable fracture, involving two of the three malleoli (often the distal fibula and medial malleolus of the tibia) usually needing the ORIF (Open Reduction and Internal Fixation), a surgical procedure, to stabilize the joint during healing.

live story! I read all about it in *TV Guide!* The guy was in bed with this woman, making whoopee, and *her dog* tried to pull him off of her by his foot, so she got the ax to kill the dog, but she missed and chopped off his foot!"

"No!" "No way!" gasped the people in the room, all except for Ms. Griffin, who was dumbfounded by this display.

Just then, two maintenance men came in the room, asking "'No' what? We're just here to change the light bulbs." Immediately they were filled in on all the gory details of the TV show. As one maintenance man extended his pole to change the ceiling bulb, he added, "But, did you know that the guy what lost his foot was not married to the woman, and her *real* husband got home early. Yeah, he heard them going at it, and *he* let the dog in. Yeah, and my sister has a friend whose cousin works down at the TV station, and she said that next week, the ax lady is gonna say that she was defending herself from a rapist, that's why she chopped his foot off!" As he said this, the near end of his pole smacked Ms. Griffin's casted foot, and she yelped out loud.

As the group muttered to each other, oblivious to Ms. Griffin, the physical therapist joined the gaggle, "Whose foot? Not this one's?"

"No, no, on TV last night," they all filled her in on the sex-canine-*BKA*[2] show.

"Oh yeah," she said, as she measured Ms. Griffin for crutches, "but I heard that, in real life, that dude is trying to sell his story to some tabloid. He said he's gonna sue the lady, and he's gonna say that the dog dragged him in the house, and the dog pulled his clothes off, and he was just an innocent bystander!"

"No friggin' way!"

---

[2] BKA: Acronym for "below the knee amputation," a surgical procedure where the leg is amputated, sparing the knee joint.

"Unbelievable!" they each exclaimed, as they left the room, some pantomiming being dragged by a dog. She could hear more details of the dismemberment story echoing off the halls outside as the troupe left her room.

Ms. Griffin sat there, wondering if her medical needs would be eclipsed by bizarre TV programs the entire time she was here. She had visions of Allen Funt and the old black and white *Candid Camera* TV show, wondering if what just happened in her room was videotaped for someone's amusement later.

She also shuddered as she thought of the "invisible treatment," a psychological torture some prison guards have used to break the will of their prisoners. She did not talk very much during the rest of her time at Cottonwood Acres. And, she worked hard at her physical therapy, so as to make her stay as short as possible.

### Where's the Love?

Well, how was Ms. Griffin's care? Technically, it was adequate. She was safely transported to her convalescent center and was placed in a clean room. She had her vitals signs checked promptly, was visited by her nurse and physical therapist shortly after arrival, and even had her light bulbs changed without having to ask. Okay, so she got her ankle banged once, but no real harm was done. Accidents do happen. So, what's the problem?

The problem is that Ms. Griffin was a non-entity. She did not really exist. She was transparent.

This should **never** happen.

**Where's the Compassion?** Compassion is the core of caring. Compassion flows from our desire to relieve suffering. Compassion is altruistic. It takes extraordinary patience and deep, loving compassion to work in any extended care facility, or nursing home.

Ms. Griffin's care, or her lack of care, may seem comical, but it's really sad. Not once did a caregiver speak to her or ask her questions or even listen to her. Her *body* was cared for, but not her, as a person.

The missing compassion is obvious. No one even tried to empathize with her. No one ministered to her. Most obviously, no one attended to her.

Surely, we say, "I could never behave so callously! If I was at Cottonwood Acres, I would show my compassion for Ms. Griffin!" But remember, it is *very* easy to ignore someone. If we ask ourselves, in the last day or two, have we failed to return a warm greeting with equal warmth? Not answered a ringing phone? Finished some paperwork before answering a call light? Brushed off the questions from children or elderly people? Not held an elevator for someone? If we answer "yes" to any of these, are we any better than the caregivers at Cottonwood Acres?

**Where's the Respect?** Is there anything more rude than ignoring someone? Ignoring a person is perhaps the worst thing one human can do to another. It's worse than insulting them, worse than hating them, worse than cursing them. If we really want to show contempt, we ignore them. Disregard them. Dismiss them. Offer them no consideration. Remember:

> *"The opposite of love is not hate, it is indifference."*
> —Elie Wiesel

The behavior of these caregivers demonstrates "burnout" at its worst. It's true; the demands on health care providers who work in long-term care facilities, that is, nursing homes, are greater than the demands on most other caregivers. The patients tend to be needy, the families demanding, and death is always nearby. Even if we place ourselves in their shoes, and imagine working with an endless sea of cognitively impaired people, stroke patients, Alzheimer's patients, etc., we must ask, is ignoring a patient the best that we can offer? Even if conversations with patients are difficult, the chores endless and menial, and the rewards few, caregivers still need to provide care. While we all must budget our time with our patients, *every minute of patient contact is sacred*. The worst job in the world never gives us permission to be rude.

Let's look at some specific mistakes. The patient was called by a medical slang term: "walkie-talkie." A "walkie-talkie" refers to any person who has a disability, but who is not impaired to the point of being unable to speak or unable to ambulate. Using any slang is discourteous. It's more discourteous to *call* a patient a slang name, and still worse to call them a slang name directly in front of the them! This is extremely offensive.

We discussed how everyone ignored Ms. Griffin. Completely. Ms. Griffin had more medical knowledge than her nurse did about her own condition, and yet the nurse paid no attention to that information. The aide did not ask permission to check vitals signs, nor did she say what she was doing, nor why she was doing it. Furthermore, just like the others, the housekeeper, the security guard and maintenance men failed to introduce themselves, and failed to offer any help with any questions Ms. Griffin might have had.

What is most worrisome is that Ms. Griffin was *talked about*, right in front of her, but never *spoken to*. The caregivers would ask each other about the new resident, as if they were discussing some new furniture. Although she was right there, no one even bothered to ask Ms. Griffin a single question. This is as bad as it gets.

To add to her indignity, Ms. Griffin was not invited to join their conversation. Needless to say, the conversation was not of a topic in which Ms. Griffin would *want* to participate. It is almost unbelievable that caregivers would discuss *any* TV show in a patient's room, especially such a vile and ridiculous program. Furthermore, near obscene language was used ("making whoopee," "goin' at it" and "friggin'"), which should never occur within earshot of a patient.

We would never behave so rudely, would we?

**Where is the Humility?** Similarly, the team thought so highly of themselves that they did not acknowledge Ms. Griffin's attempts to communicate. This lack of humility is also very bad. As a teacher, Ms. Griffin has done more to benefit society than all of her caregivers combined. They should be in awe of Ms. Griffin, and be proud to take care of her, not ignore her.

The painful irony of Ms. Griffin's situation is that she is a bright, articulate woman, who is ignored by the people around her. They are not even discussing her care: the cluster of dimwits who invade her room are rehashing an inane TV program! The conversation is so far below Ms. Griffin's intellectual level that she can't even interject! Being upstaged by trash TV need never happen to our patients.

## Do the Right Thing

What would we do? First, we would introduce ourselves. Any caregiver in the room could have broken the cycle of irrelevant chatter by simply introducing themselves to Ms. Griffin. By refocusing our attention towards the patient, we force other caregivers around us to recognize their own impoliteness. This gives them a face-saving way of attending to the patient. Once a caregiver becomes aware of their rude behavior, they will often over-correct, and spend extra time fawning over the patient.

Alternatively, when we enter her room and notice an inappropriate conversation, instead of jumping in and telling our part of the story, we could softly announce, "That's interesting, but we are here to care for Ms. Griffin, so why don't we continue this conversation later?" This re-focuses the caregivers back towards the patient. However, we should not be too self-righteous when we do this. We don't want to humiliate our peers. It's just a matter of time before *we* are the one being re-directed.

Another approach is the bullhorn method. We just shout, "Everyone be quiet!" I have actually done this! During my training, a trauma patient's arrival in the Emergency Department would draw a huge number of people to the resuscitation room, many of whom had little to do with direct patient care. As the din of activity grew louder, I would stand up on a footstool and shout, "If you are not directly involved in this patient's care, please wait outside!" Extraneous people would leave, and the quality of the patient's care was improved.

We should never ignore patients. Comatose patients, patients under anesthesia, catatonic[3] patients all deserve our respect. Our conversations with these patients will be quite different from other conversations. However, just as we tell visitors to talk freely to their unresponsive loved ones, we too should interact respectfully with *all* our patients. There are many cases of patients under anesthesia or in a coma, who wake up, and can describe conversations that took place in their presence while they were unresponsive.

I once met a young woman who worked as a nurse's aide in a nursing home (the politically correct terms are "patient assistant technician" and "long term care facility"). Her job is perhaps one of the most menial in healthcare. Yet, she was happy and proud of her job. She told me, "These are some of the most spiritual people I have ever met. They teach me so

---

[3] Catatonic: Psychiatric syndrome associated with lack of movement, rigidity, and/or stupor.

much. I love them all." On that day, this woman taught *me* a great deal.

## Practice Makes Perfect

Tomorrow, give your very best attention to a patient. Let them know, without any doubt, that you are completely focused upon them. Lock eyes with them a few times. Repeat back what they have said. Your attention shows your sincere interest. Both of you will be better off for it.

Whenever we have to discuss anything besides our patient, or do anything that does not involve them, we must excuse our self first. Remember, "Excuse me," lets them know that we are now diverting our attention from them. Our patients will realize how focused on them we are. "Excuse me," is very compassionate and respectful.

When we are with a patient, *they* are what's important. Let them know this by listening, making eye contact, and saying, "excuse me" often. Remember, our patient is our *raison d'etre* (our *reason for being*.)

## Give a Gift

When you greet someone, include their name in your greeting. For example, "Hi, Ms. Griffin, I'm Dr. Diering..." Invoke their name frequently and warmly. As Dale Carnegie said, "Remember, that a person's name is to that person the sweetest and most important sound in any language."

The more you say it, the more likely you will remember it. And the more your patient hears it, the more they will appreciate you.

# CHAPTER 14

# Mr. Mebae's Lesson

*A*rthur Mebae was intoxicated. He had finished his house-painting job early, stopped at The Gambler, his local bar, and settled in for a good drunk. When he ran out of money, he carefully negotiated the half-mile drive home.

However, he never quite made it. He managed to park on the driveway, but he slipped off the stairs to his trailer. Without a handrail, he landed on the ground. He found himself twisted up, sitting on the azalea.

Now, Arthur Mebae was in pain, as well as intoxicated. When he was finished swearing, he sat there, puzzling over the bloody, swollen ankle before him. "Wow," he thought, "Why does it hurt so much? And look so funny? And where is the blood coming from?"

His family came out of the trailer to find him sitting on the azalea bush. They knew this was worse than usual.

His wife, and his two teenage sons, had lived with an alcoholic long enough to distinguish drunken stupidity from a serious problem.

Arthur Mebae's sons helped him up and to the family station wagon, and his wife got some towels to wrap around his bleeding ankle. She thought she saw bone sticking out, and she almost vomited. But she held back. It was 3:30 PM.

During the ride to the hospital, Arthur Mebae nodded off intermittently, occasionally complaining about his wife's driving, or the condition of their town, or anything else that came to mind. He was reasonably good-natured when intoxicated, and otherwise a good man. His family, painfully co-dependent, loved him very deeply.

Upon arrival at the ER, Mr. Mebae was triaged and taken to a room fairly quickly, since an open fracture is a relatively urgent problem. The ER physician, Dr. Peter Dant, promptly and thoroughly evaluated Mr. Mebae, and told the family he would need surgery to fix his broken ankle. As he left, he said he'd be back.

The nurse started Mr. Mebae's IV line, gave him 2 milligrams of morphine sulfate, and hung antibiotics.[1] The radiology tech shot some X-rays. Mr. Mebae snored.

Mr. Mebae's family stared from across the room at him, wondering if they should try to comfort him, wondering what they should do. They pitied him. They also pitied themselves. They were worrying about these new bills, and the loss of his income. His wife was beginning to hope this may be an opportunity to get her husband to look at his drinking, and maybe even stop. His sons were embarrassed, as usual. But they were also in pain, for their mother, and for their father. Mr. Mebae snored.

When Dr. Dant returned, he had a small entourage. Mr. Mebae's family backed against the walls. Dr. Dant crowded into the room with the nurse, two nursing students, another younger doctor and a paramedic student. Dr. Dant puffed himself up a bit, and began.

---

[1] An open fracture, i.e., a fracture where the broken bone has been exposed to air, is a surgical emergency. The standard of care usually includes IV antibiotics.

"Here we have an open fracture, I suspect a *compound fracture*[2] of the distal *tib-fib*[3]...we'll see exactly when the X-rays are developed. Although this bleeding draws your attention, it is imperative that you, as health care providers, notice everything else that is pertinent about this patient's presentation. What else do you observe?" The ad hoc class was silent, unsure what Dr. Dant was thinking.

He continued. "Let us begin at the head, and work our way down. Here, at his head, we see disheveled unwashed hair, several old bruises and abrasions. What do you notice about his nose? Perhaps a little red, a few prominent blood vessels? And his breath? Does anyone smell alcohol?"

Mr. Mebae's family was stunned. "So he doesn't wash his hair every day, who does?" his eldest son thought. "Of course he smells of alcohol, he's been drinking, why do you think he fell and got hurt?" his younger son thought. "Well, nobody's perfect, and you're no rose yourself, doctor," his wife thought. But no one spoke.

Dr. Dant continued. "This patient has all the signs of a chronic alcoholic!" he professed, as if this were some type of profound revelation. "Notice the *JVD*,[4] here, probably indicative of portal hypertension.[5] His liver is palpable 2 centimeters below the costal margin, and, if I am not mistaken, these varicosities around his umbilicus are early *caput medusae*!"[6] He proudly held back Mr. Mebae's sheet to reveal his

---

[2] Compound fracture: Open fracture; the broken bone is exposed to air, and bacteria.

[3] Tib-fib: The bones of the leg, tibia and fibula (distal to the thigh bone, the femur).

[4] JVD: Jugular venous distention, suggesting high venous pressures.

[5] Portal hypertension: elevated venous pressure in the liver.

[6] Caput Medusae: Enlarged or varicose veins, around the umbilicus, or belly button.

abdomen. He was acting like Sherlock Holmes, and this abdomen was some clue in a bizarre forensic case.

"Yes, this is no ordinary compound fracture, indeed, this is a complicated case! Management of his liver dysfunction, his probable bleeding diathesis and the expected EtOH[7] withdrawal syndrome dramatically complicates his course!" Dr. Dant continued his pontifications as he meandered out of the room, his rapt audience following closely behind. Mr. Mebae snored.

Mr. Mebae's family was devastated. They could deduce from the doctor's revelations that their loved one was in trouble, yet they had no idea what it all meant, how serious it was going to be, or if there was anything they could do.

They each slowly drifted back towards his bed. Mrs. Mebae held his hand while her husband slept, tears running down her cheeks. Her sons tried to comfort her, but they were just as distressed as she was, and just as confused. They stared down at their drunk, injured father, hating him, loving him, and worrying about him. Mr. Mebae snored.

They took turns crying until he was out of surgery four hours later.

**Where's the Love?**

Is there anything wrong with using a patient to make a teaching point? Some patients enjoy being the center of attention, even if they do not understand their illness. Sometimes, patients receive good second opinions when they are the subjects of focused teaching rounds. Yet sometimes, patients are used as circus monkeys, doing little pathophysiological tricks for the professor's audience. Which was Mr. Mebae?

---

[7] EtOH: Ethanol or ethyl alcohol, the type of alcohol people drink.

Mr. Mebae's care was adequate. He had his fracture evaluated, and he did get pain medication, antibiotics and X-rays before an orthopedic consult.

However, the teaching lesson was denigrating and insulting, to Mr. Mebae, as well as to his family. It would have been nice to see some compassion, some respect and some humility. Love was missing from Dr. Dant's care.

We should give Dr. Dant credit. Educating fellow care-givers is an admirable and challenging goal. We are all responsible to teach. We should applaud Dr. Dant for taking time to teach his pupils.

However, patients are not specimens. Patients are people who need love. While patients often feel that being a subject for teaching is a silver lining to their illness, they provide us this service at the risk of *becoming* their diagnosis.

**Where's the Compassion?** While Dr. Dant showed compassion to Mr. Mebae by providing some morphine, this is a minimal effort. Clearly, the patient who needs attention is Mr. Mebae's family.

The family felt alone. They desperately needed compassion. Unfortunately, they were ignored. Dr. Dant completely forgot to empathize with them, and minister to them with some warm attention. Instead, they were subjected to his self-aggrandizing ranting about manifestations of chronic alcoholism.

Dr. Dant was so excited about Mr. Mebae's physical exam findings that he forgot about Mr. Mebae's family. Dr. Dant is usually quite compassionate. However, he lost sight of his patients, the Mebae family, in his zeal to share Mr. Mebae's signs of alcoholism with the other caregivers.

**Where's the Respect?** Was Dr. Dant courteous? Did he praise the family's care? Was he honest?

Dr. Dant did not even introduce himself to Mr. Mebae's worried family. Worse yet, he did not ask permission for trainees to meet Mr. Mebae, nor did he offer the family the opportunity to excuse themselves and avoid the embarrassment of having their loved one dissected, as if under a microscope, right in front of them.

Dr. Dant states, "Yes, this is no ordinary compound fracture, indeed, this is a complicated case!" Mr. Mebae is not a person, he is a "compound fracture" and a "complicated case." This is very convenient; suddenly, there is no patient, no family, and no sadness. Although easy, this is one of the worst things a caregiver can do: define a person by their problem.

When we distill a human being into their medical problem, we *lose* the person. This is rude, almost as bad as ignoring a person. It takes almost no additional energy to say, "This person with a compound fracture..." or "This patient with complications of chemical dependency..." thereby *including* the person in the diagnosis.

Although his plan of care includes treating Mr. Mebae's alcohol-induced problems, the issue is, where was Dr. Dant's *focus*? What was important to Dr. Dant? Although Mr. Mebae's medical care was important, this is the minimum standard of care which Mr. Mebae should expect.

We have to wonder, is Dr. Dant a show-off? Is his own agenda more important than his patient? He shows off his knowledge, shows off his new patient, and shows off his teaching ability. He shows off everything except his respect and his compassion.

Being a show-off is never respectful.

**Where's the Humility?** Dr. Dant *is* a show-off. He wants attention focused on him. His patient is there to make him look good. Dr. Dant is proud of his knowledge, and proud of his specimen. Dr. Dant is not humble.

It's not bad to want to be the center of attention every now and then. Everyone wants to look good. We cannot be angry with Dr. Dant for wanting to show off his knowledge and his observations. However, this display is at someone else's expense. A self-centered, self-aggrandizing, self-important egotist, Dr. Dant failed to show humility with this patient.

The family is the patient, too. There is never a reason to ignore them. Regardless of whether or not the patient is alert, or why the patient is unresponsive, the caregiver's responsibility is to provide quality health care, *which includes comforting and educating the family*. In fact, Mr. Mebae seems to require very little direct physician interaction. Dr. Dant should have used some of his time to console family, and teach them about the probable hospital course.

Unfortunately, it seems that Dr. Dant is too concerned with this opportunity to look good. He was spraying medical jargon around like an insect sprays pheromones. He did not even bother to define these terms to the students who were present, let alone teach the family about complications of alcoholism. He focused on himself.

Not only did Dr. Dant fail to translate his lecture for the family, he skipped admiring them, too. He was not impressed at all. He should have complimented the family on their pre-hospital care, and thanked them for allowing him to do his little lecture.

Dr. Dant showed no graciousness. He never sat down. And, he should have apologized to the family for using jargon in front of them.

## Do the Right Thing

What would we do? Once life-and-limb saving treatments have been instituted, what else could we do to make this visit to the hospital a little less painful for the Mebae's?

If we were Dr. Dant, a simple introduction, offering the family chairs, and complimenting them on their pre-hospital care, would be a lot. We would demonstrate our humility and simultaneously we would offer praise and respect for their actions.

During the history and physical exam, we would acknowledge how difficult it must be for them to see their loved one in such a state, showing our compassion.

We could ask directly, and with concern, about the extent of the patient's alcohol abuse, and introduce the topic of alcoholism and recovery, all in a *nonjudgmental fashion*. For example, while Mr. Mebae snores, we could say to the family, "I smell alcohol.... Has Mr. Mebae been drinking today? Is this common for him? Are you concerned he may be an alcoholic?" Or, we could say, "Is Mr. Mebae a big drinker? I ask because he shows some signs of chronic alcohol use." Alternatively, we could ask him. For example, "Are you a big drinker? Don't be offended, I ask everyone..." Under these circumstances, discussing alcoholism *as a disease* can be the first step towards recovery, recovery for the whole family.

Of course, we'd ask permission before we'd present Mr. Mebae as a case. Since the students and other caregivers are not directly involved in his care, parading Mr. Mebae's pathologies in front of them may be a breech of confidentiality. Perhaps we'd ask, "Do you mind if some students examine your husband as well? He has several unique attributes. You may stay here or wait outside, whatever you'd prefer." Or, to Mr. Mebae, "May I bring in some students to examine you, too? They could learn a great deal from you."

Needless to say, we'd *respectfully* describe Mr. Mebae's exam findings. For any illness, it is sometimes helpful to include the family in the group of pupils. This helps remove any doubt about the diagnosis: Seeing is believing.

While Dr. Dant failed to show love in every possible way, we would never argue that *teaching* be omitted. In teaching institutions, patients and their families understand and accept that there will be students, residents and trainees at various levels, and that some aspects of care may be longer or belabored accordingly. (If patients desire no student interactions, they need to be at a facility that has no teaching or training mandate.)

However, the presence of healthcare professionals-in-training does not preclude caring with love. With students, the teacher has an even stronger obligation to *model* appropriate behavior. Just like an actor on a stage, a teacher in a hospital must over-emphasize respect, humility and compassion, to amplify these attitudes for the pupils.

Clinical information will be remembered when the students learn in a respectful environment where *the patient* is the center of attention. Recalling clinical data is easier if the context in which it is learned is rich with such cues and mnemonics. Compassionate, patient-centered interactions will ensure that Mr. Mebae will not be an abstract lesson, easily forgotten.

Suppose we are one of the pupils Dr. Dant invites into Mr. Mebae's room? What can we do? It may be up to *us* to model appropriate behavior for Dr. Dant. We may need to introduce our self to the family. This is a reminder to the other caregivers that the family and patient must remain the center of attention. Perhaps, as in the famous movie, *Patch Adams*, we could merely ask the patient (or the family) their name. Before leaving the room, we may need to ask Dr. Dant how these findings impact the family, or what services are available in the hospital for alcoholics and their families.

Questions guided by love will refocus the group's attention on the *people* involved, not just the pathology. It is easy to keep a group's focus on the patient. For example, holding our patient's hand while we listen to them, making eye contact, or offering to get something for them, proves to patients *they* are the focus of our attention.

**Practice Makes Perfect**

Practice validating people. No matter what someone has done, say, "Nice job," or "Beautiful," or "Thanks for that," before you say anything else, especially if you are going to disagree!

Try to remember to be encouraging. We don't need to agree with their words or their actions, and we don't have to thank them for anger or being upset. But, it's really nice when we acknowledge the intensity or feelings behind their actions.

If someone has done something really inappropriate, or if they say something that bothers you, stop. Stop to figure out what their intention may be. Give them the benefit of the doubt.

Say something like, "I think we both have the same goals," or " I agree with your interest in this problem," or "You obviously feel very strongly about this." Let them know that their thinking, their rationale and their intentions seem to be good ones, and are similar to yours. Worry about teaching or correcting them *after* validating them.

Remember, at work, you can never win any argument. You may disagree, but don't argue.

**Give a Gift**

Give the gift of appreciation. Express your gratefulness for someone's patience, for their understanding that you are learning, or just for their willingness to be with you today. Thank someone for their trust in you. Thank them for allowing you to care for them.

Your appreciation is a gift. It reminds you that everyone has something to offer you. And, it will help your patients to be better patients.

# CHAPTER 15

# Mr. Leffete's Embarrassment

Ms. Jackie Buffet is a Licensed Practical Nurse at Memorial, a large community hospital. She is good at what she does, and the R.N.s with whom she works always enjoy having her on the job. She is usually bubbly and cheerful. She gets her job done. It is done efficiently, quietly and, most of the time, without help.

Ms. Buffet cares for inpatients in their rooms. She checks vital signs, assists with medication administration, delivers meal trays, helps with toileting, and changes linens. She enters a room with a smile and a well-rehearsed greeting, such as "It's not the Ritz, but it beats the pits! How can I help?" Everyone seems comfortable with her.

Mr. Paul Leffete is a patient in room 219. Mr. Leffete, a retired wastewater processing plant engineer, is seventy-four years old, although he could pass for eighty-four. Or ninety-four.

Mr. Leffete is very tired. He is tired of working so hard to breathe, tired of taking so many medicines, tired of being told what to do. Sometimes, he is just tired of living. He is hospitalized now for congestive heart failure, COPD[1] and hyponatremia,[2] and will likely be going back to his apartment at the Vets Home, where he lives, later today.

Mr. Leffete is a former smoker, and his fingers are still stained by years of tobacco abuse. Although he is not demented, his cognitive ability is ... slowed. It takes him longer than average to comprehend and respond to most conversation. However, he is trusting, undemanding, and modest. He has tolerated the indignities of this hospitalization rather well.

Mr. Leffete, like many men his age, is occasionally incontinent of urine. For Mr. Leffete, it is urge incontinence. He feels the urge to void, when his bladder is filling. However, the urge to urinate is followed almost immediately by a bladder spasm. He will fight the spasm (the spasm of his bladder trying to empty), with a *perineal*[3] squeeze, to tighten up his sphincter. However, he only has a minute or so before the bladder spasms become quite painful. Sometimes, he loses the battle to hold his urine. At home, he wears incontinence briefs, but actually only wets them about every other day. He has refused to take medications that might help, since he feels he takes too many pills already. He is proud of his remaining ability to keep himself dry, since some of his peers have lost that ability.

During this hospitalization, Mr. Leffete's therapy has consisted mainly of bronchodilators, oxygen and *diuretics*[4]...

---

[1] COPD: Chronic obstructive pulmonary disease, i.e., a decreased ability to breathe (mainly exhale) and exchange oxygen.

[2] Hyponatremia: Low serum sodium.

[3] Perineum (Perineal): The area between the thighs, from the pubic region in front to the tailbone in the back.

[4] Diuretics: Medications, which cause the kidneys to reduce water retention, increasing urine output. (Furosemide (Lasix) and metolazone (Zaroxolyn) are diuretics.)

large doses of diuretics. His doctor increased his furosemide dose and added metolazone to his medication regimen. Naturally, he had a urethral catheter, since he was passing two to three liters of urine a day. With the catheter in place, he never had to run to the bathroom. His perineal muscles went on vacation! However, those muscles became weak, without a full bladder and urges to void.

Today, Mr. Leffete's oxygen was discontinued, and his urethral catheter was removed, in anticipation of discharge. Unfortunately, no order for cross clamping[5] the catheter tube was written yesterday. Since his perineal muscles have weakened, he lost his ability to hold his urine.

His weakened perineum plus the diuretics have made for an embarrassing day. Now, he has wet his bed for the third time. He was so upset with himself that he waited an hour before signaling the nurse's station.

Ms. Buffet was almost expecting this third episode. She bounded into room 219 to find Mr. Leffete soaked, and whistled aloud. "Pauly, honey, if you want to go for a swim, tell the doctor and go with him!" Mr. Leffete blushed in painful embarrassment. As Ms. Buffet said this, she was lowering the head of the bed. She pressed the remote button with one hand and pushed the head of the bed down with the other. She did not help him out of the bed this time. She did not ask permission, or warn Mr. Leffete of this change in posture. For Ms. Buffet, it was natural, since flattening the bed made the sheet change faster and easier.

Besides, she thought, he brought all this upon himself, with that dirty cigarette habit.

Mr. Leffete's lungs still have some mild vascular engorgement, and he has not fully recovered his baseline oxy-

---

[5] Cross-clamp: Stopping the flow of urine through the catheter tube for three to four hours at a time allows the bladder to fill and empty normally, even though the catheter is still in place.

gen exchange capability. In fact, *orthopnea*[6] has been typical for Mr. Leffete for weeks. Laying down flat causes him severe shortness of breath. During this linen change, he laid flat quietly. However, the reason for his silence quickly changed from embarrassment to hypoxia.

Ms. Buffet, in her goal-oriented zeal, did not notice this. Once the bed was flat, Ms. Buffet grabbed the draw sheet, and spun Mr. Leffete up onto his side. Mr. Leffete gasped, a real gasp. What little air he had been getting was knocked out of him by the jolt. Ms. Buffet chatted away with her standard humor, "Aah, Pauly, look at this bed, you could join the Peace Corp tomarrah and go and irrigate the Sahara!"

With his dwindling cognitive abilities, Mr. Leffete wished he were dead. His oxygen saturation quickly dropped below seventy percent, rendering him desperately uncomfortable. Higher level functioning, like speech, was nearly impossible.

The sheets were stripped, new ones tucked and his gown changed in short order. Ms. Buffet had Mr. Leffete up (and exchanging oxygen again) in no time.

Ms. Buffet quipped as she walked out the door, "Next time you take a pee, please wait till after three!" Three o'clock, of course, quitting time for Ms. Buffet.

Mr. Leffete was still gasping for air, but his upright posture permitted him to reverse the cyanosis,[7] which had just started to color his lips. He was dizzy. He worked hard to regain the lost oxygen. It would be hours before he was back to his pre-bed-change level. In fact, he looked so out-of-breath on afternoon rounds that his physician put him back on continuous oxygen, and delayed his discharge for an extra day.

---

[6]Orthopnea: The influence of posture on breathing; sitting up is easier to breathe.

[7] Cyanosis: Blue color of the skin and mucous membranes due to low oxygen saturation.

Mr. Leffete's depression worsened as well.

Ms. Buffet would never know that she had contributed to a man's illness, as well as his depression. In fact, she would never think of Mr. Leffete again, oblivious to any wrongdoing on her part. For Ms. Buffet, there really aren't any patients. She feels that patients belong to doctors and RNs; for Ms. Buffet, there are just room numbers, chores, and a captive audience for her witty chatter.

## Where's the Love?

In analyzing Ms. Buffet's behavior, do we see any terrible mistakes? Isn't her efficiency worth a little patient discomfort? Ms. Buffet did not really injure Mr. Leffete, did she? Besides, Mr. Leffete probably won't remember the offense anyway, so what difference does it make?

Ms. Buffet's behavior was deplorable, and on several levels. Just because Ms. Buffet does an excellent job, she does not have the right to abuse patients.

Ms. Buffet may have been efficient, but she lacked compassion. She was cheery, but she lacked respect for the patient. She even lost points on humility.

**Where's the Compassion?** There is no trade-off between efficiency and compassion. Anyone who does a good job can do a better job, by adding personal warmth.

Ms. Buffet knows Mr. Leffete, and she is aware of the patient's shame and embarrassment at having wet his bed. Where was her empathy? Where was her caring touch? Instead of compassion, he got impatience. Her impatience was worse because of her prejudice towards smokers.

There is no place for prejudice in healthcare.

Ms. Buffet seemed in too much of a hurry to pay attention to Mr. Leffete. Since she did not attend to him, she did not notice his embarrassment. She could not empathize with what she did not notice. She did not feel that she needed to be comforting, since she did not notice his shame. Ms. Buffet cared for a wet bed. She did not care for a person.

**Where's the Respect?** Ms. Buffet was disrespectful on several levels. She addressed the patient by his first name, as well as the condescending "honey." "Mr. Leffete" is the only name appropriate, unless they agreed beforehand to first names.

She was also rough. Although we use our strength all the time, unnecessary *roughness* is abuse. It doesn't matter if Ms. Buffet did not *intend* to be abusive, she abused her patient. (We question her innocence when we see her disdain for smokers.) As we said, the healthcare setting is no place for personal prejudices! It does not matter how much Mr. Leffete is responsible for his own infirmity, or how much Ms. Buffet hates tobacco. The quality of our care cannot be rationed based on our personal feelings.

Ms. Buffet used toilet humor several times. Humor is a very delicate and risky tool for gaining patient trust and respect. However, *toilet* humor is rude, and demonstrates one's immaturity and apathy about the other person's feelings. In an environment where urine and stool and flatus[8] may be monitored and are important signs of health, making jokes about them may allow patients to see these bodily functions as unimportant, a source of humor or embarrassment. It's true, not all patients understand medical terms for bodily functions; to be understood, we may need to use appropriate idioms or slang to refer to these bodily functions. However, all discussion of bodily functions should be with respect for the importance of those functions.

**Where's the Humility?** It may seem that Ms. Buffet has little reason to behave with humility. After all, isn't her job one of the lowest on the hierarchy, such that she is humbled every day?

---

[8] Flatus: Gas released from the rectum; "fart."

On the contrary, I feel that since she is one of the best LPNs, it is her duty to demonstrate humility. Ms. Buffet needs to focus more on her patients and less on herself.

Ms. Buffet is proud of her witty little rhymes. The rhymes are good icebreakers. However, they can emotionally distance her from her patients. (This distance allows her to work unimpeded by empathy.) While she is focusing on her witty verses, she does not have to think of the pain and anguish that is all around her. She does not focus on her patients. Further, when her patients are elderly, or cognitively slow, these rhymes may confuse them and silence them. While they are trying to figure out what she said, they cannot ask meaningful questions.

Any overused statements are "canned," as in, out of a can. Canned phrases are not just rhymes or jokes, they are anything memorized and regurgitated. Canned products are for mass consumption. Canned phrases are never personalized. Canned, repetitive or overused lectures prevent us from establishing rapport. They prevent us from asking our patients meaningful questions. Canned phrases prevent us from tailoring what we say to our patient.

Anything can be canned, from instructions on filling out paperwork, to orientations to the floor, to descriptions of surgical procedures. Although it *is* important for us to explain something completely, it is equally important to be certain our audience hears what we have said. Canned phrases frequently go right over the patient's head.

### Do the Right Thing

If we were Ms. Buffet, how could we still care for Mr. Leffete, and yet change the linens efficiently? We could plan our interaction as we walk towards Mr. Leffete's room. We know he is modest, and we can enter the room with comforting words of reassurance. For example, "Don't worry, everyone wets the bed here." Or, "It's nothing to be ashamed of, I am just glad you are getting the extra fluid off." Any soft words, words that show we understand how he must feel, would be helpful. Most importantly, we'd show that we do not hold the incontinence against him, that it is *no big deal*.

Ms. Buffet's lack of grace should inspire us to apologize a lot. We might say, "I am sorry you are wet.... I am sorry you need help to get dry.... I am sorry you have to endure such indignities.... I am sorry you are in the hospital." We would humbly show our empathy for his situation.

Maybe we'd comfort him, without the confusing rhymes. For example, we could show we understand his feelings, this third episode of incontinence today. A simple statement, such as, "Oh, it must be awful to go through this today, and with strangers!" would touch Mr. Leffete's heart. Such sympathetic words would show him that we understand how he feels.

Perhaps we'd begin our task by reminding Mr. Leffete exactly what needed to be done. When we explain our plans to our patient, we allow him to complain or object, and this allows him to offer ways to customize the procedure so as to accommodate him. If we listened to him, he might have been able to explain how he'd need supplemental oxygen in order to lay flat.

If we were conversing with Mr. Leffete, we'd *notice* that he suddenly stopped speaking when he was laid flat. We'd suspect something was wrong. We'd immediately return the bed to upright, we'd summon a registered nurse, or we'd put the oxygen back on. Whatever our decision, the sudden stop in conversation would be important medical information. Ms. Buffet missed this completely. Although the sheets may have taken a few seconds longer to change, we may have saved our patient an extra day in the hospital.

Some things we do cause discomfort. Whether it is changing linens, drawing blood, or placing a chest tube, that discomfort can be greatly reduced by warm words and a soft touch. While pain may be unavoidable, comforting our patients should never be avoided.

## Practice Makes Perfect

Remember, our face, our hands, and our voices communicate our message. Our words are merely punctuation for that message.

For the next week, at least once a day, put yourself in your patient's shoes. Listen to a patient's words, to their groans, to their facial expressions. When you think you really know what they are communicating to you, see how *you* feel. Do you want to run away? Do you dismiss what they must be feeling? Do you want to fix them? Then, check again what *they* feel. Then, what do *you* feel? Go back and forth a few times. Don't worry ... you'll be using your *limbic system*[9] to do this, and you'll still be able to think.

If you are honest with yourself, you will notice that sometimes you can be very accurate at identifying what someone else feels. You may also notice that, at these times, you are able to *feel what they feel*. This is empathy. If you do not ignore your recognition that you feel what they feel, and if you do not try to fix them, you will notice that your *responses* will be beautifully customized to your patient. They will be amazed at your ability to understand exactly what they feel.

This takes practice. This also demands that you can accurately identify what *you* are feeling at any given moment. Unfortunately, some of us have spent years suppressing and disavowing our own feelings, in an effort to avoid feeling the pain of other's suffering. However, with a little work, you

---

[9] Limbic system: The emotional centers of our brain, consisting mainly of subcortical structures, such as the hippocampus, the amygdala, and hypothalamic connections.

will feel the rich benefits of again identifying your emotional reactions to other people.

## Give a Gift

Give the gift of freeing someone from embarrassment. No matter what your patient may have done, let them know it's *no big deal*. Say, "People vomit on me all the time … you should have seen me this morning!" Or, "Don't worry, everyone's stool smells bad … we are used to it!" Or, "It's no big deal!" or "That was a good one … keep it up!" Or, "It's perfectly normal to release gas," or "What you did is fine; it's nothing we haven't seen a hundred times!" Or some personalized phrase. We want to acknowledge a person's embarrassing action, and then *make it okay*. We can *free them* from their embarrassment.

# CHAPTER
## 16

# Ms. Zingle's Target

Ms. Zingle knew something. Something was wrong. She was sweaty. And a little shaky.

She was not surprised, though. She was not concerned. She knew she had not been eating properly. For the last two … or three? days. She was actually proud of her control over her appetite. At last maybe she could do something right. Maybe she could lose some weight.

Ms. Zingle knows she is obese. She knows obesity causes diabetes. She understands that she might be able to stop the insulin injections if she could just lose one or two hundred pounds. She also realizes that the depression for which she is being treated would improve if she weren't five foot six inches tall and 369 pounds.

However, right now, she is not thinking of any of that. Her blood sugar is 31, well below her usual 200. Instead of heeding her body's warning signs of hypoglycemia (the fragmented thoughts, the shaky, sweaty feelings) by gulping orange juice, she hesitated. She hesitated just long enough to cross the line. She crossed beyond being able to help herself. She just sat there.

Without her usual snacks, the 60 units of insulin she gave herself earlier that morning, as prescribed, was more than she needed.

She was drifting. Drifting in a small boat. Going into a long, foggy tunnel. As the fog of hypoglycemia enveloped her, she stopped thinking. She just sat there. Shaking. She could not worry. She slowly drifted towards insulin shock.

However, Ms. Zingle's insulin did not know nor care that she had not been eating. The insulin does not care that her blood glucose level is dangerously low. The insulin is doing its job. The insulin does not care that there is not enough glucose to go around. The insulin turns on the glucose vacuums in Ms. Zingle's cells, all except her brain cells, and those other cells suck up all the glucose. Ms. Zingle's brain is starved for glucose. Ms. Zingle's brain is running on empty. No fuel for the brain, no normal brain function. Without a normal supply of glucose in her blood stream, her brain is shutting down.

So, Ms. Zingle just sits there.

Ms. Zingle's daughter, Latesha, knew the moment she walked into the kitchen that her mother was having an insulin reaction.

Her daughter quickly mixed up some sugar with orange juice, and managed to get her mother to gulp some down. However, Latesha called 911 anyway. The ambulance carried Ms. Zingle the six blocks to the local hospital.

The paramedics did not give the usual amp of intravenous D50[1] en route, since they were unable to gain IV access in the short trip. They stopped carrying glucagon[2] last year, so the paramedics gave no treatments. They ended their report to the nurses with, "Good luck."

By the time she arrived at the hospital, the fog was clearing a little bit. The orange juice was working. A little.

---

[1] D50: Solution of 50% dextrose in water, an IV antidote for hypoglycemia.

[2] Glucagon: An antidote for hypoglycemia (low blood sugar); it's a hormone that mobilizes hepatic glycogen to raise blood sugar, and can be given intramuscularly.

Lying on the gurney, Ms. Zingle still felt like she was on a boat, but she could see through the fog now. She could see people around her. The sugar and orange juice stopped her blood glucose from falling further, but she was still far from normal. The ER doctor, Dr. Wilson, popped in briefly and said to the nurse, "Check a dex[3] and give an amp of D50 when the IV is started." Nurse Macomber got her students to measure Ms. Zingle's blood sugar. It was 39.

Nurse Macomber, with eighteen years experience in urban and suburban hospitals, recognized a difficult IV stick when she saw one, and Ms. Zingle was clearly going to be difficult. Ms. Zingle had no visible veins. However, Nurse Macomber had no intention of giving up without a fight. Nurse Macomber felt strongly that nursing students needed to learn from problem patients (especially those patients too obtunded to complain). She called in her two nursing students, and gave them a brief speech on the importance of IV access in an emergency patient. She then placed several 20 gauge angiocaths on the counter, and saw to it that each student had gloves, a rubber tourniquet and alcohol swabs.

The three of them went to work. At 39, Ms. Zingle's blood sugar is still well below the normal of 70, but high enough for her to allow some awareness. Ms. Zingle still felt the thick, gray fog all around her. The fog was heavy, but she could move some now. She could talk a little. The fog obscured her view, but she could see the serious looks on the people surrounding her. She knew she was being squeezed, pulled and rubbed.

Nurse Macomber would pull on Ms. Zingle's hand, tense the skin on the back of her hand, and feel for the hidden vein. She would point to the exact site where the vein could be best accessed. Ms. Zingle observed with curiosity, but she could

---

[3] Dex: Slang for serum glucose level. There are many rapid, bedside test kits available.

only mumble, not really ask questions. When the first needle pierced through her skin, she frowned, yelled "Ow!" and weakly tried to pull away. The movement was just enough to disrupt the needle's position in the vein, and cause the vein to bleed under the skin.

"Blew it!" growled Nurse Macomber, recognizing that the hematoma[4] formed by the extravascular blood would obscure the vessel and, for this day, ruin it for IV access. Nurse Macomber then directed the student to hold pressure with a 2x2 square of gauze as she moved to Ms. Zingle's other arm, to repeat the search-and-expose maneuvers.

Ms. Zingle was rather puzzled by all this, but she could still feel pain. And she felt it again and again, as they tried to catheterize various spots on her arms, wrists and hands. With each needle stick, she withdrew. And with each withdrawal, she blew a vein.

"Don't move!" ... "Ow!" ... "Damn!" could be heard over and over.

Besides the "don't move," none of the people in the room spoke to Ms. Zingle, although they did speak to the veins in her hands and arms. Ms. Zingle floated in and out of her foggy darkness, sometimes quite aware she was being poked, other times wondering what was going on, all the while confused as to why she was feeling the pain.

The students tried their best. First, the needle would cause pain. Then, the nurses would carefully guide the tip of the needle to where they felt the underlying vein. If there were no flash of blood, they would withdraw the needle a little bit, and change angles and move forward again, causing more pain. They would repeat this subtle maneuver over and over, until there was a flash of blood in the catheter, indicating that the tip had perforated a vein. Then, once

---

[4] Hematoma: An organized mass of blood, usually clotted, outside a blood vessel.

inside the vein, they would advance the catheter slowly, withdrawing the metal needle, leaving only the plastic catheter in the vein. But even with Nurse Macomber holding her arm, Ms. Zingle would always move just enough to dislodge the catheter before it could be taped in place.

After fifteen minutes and seven attempts at IV access, Dr. Wilson came back. He was told about the seven sticks. He frowned, and looked sternly at the nurses. Then he said, "That is disgraceful ... let me show you how a pro does it! Who'll bet me that I can get a line in this lady within three tries?"

The nurse team looked at each other, then at the doctor, and Nurse Macomber said, "You're on! If you can't get at least a 20 gauge in her within three tries, you buy us all pizza tonight!" Dr. Wilson sprang as the gauntlet was dropped. He ignored the worried look on Ms. Zingle's face as he scoured her extremities for an adequate vessel.

After six more perforations, including three on her feet, Ms. Zingle looked more obtunded, and they guessed her blood glucose was dropping again. Dr. Wilson threw up his hands, admitting defeat.

"What will it be, pepperoni?" he said, grinning, as the crew left the bay. Once outside Ms. Zingle's room, he ordered a repeat dextrostick. He said that perhaps they all failed because the patient was dehydrated. He ordered glucagon, 1 mg IM, saying, "There's more than one way to skin a cat, even a fat cat."

Latesha Zingle arrived shortly after the glucagon was given. Tears rose in her eyes at the sight of her mother decorated all over with tape and gauze. Nurse Macomber and students were gone. Latesha shook her head at her mother.

Ms. Zingle sighed and said, "I feel like a dart board in an Irish pub."

## Where's the Love?

Are we permitted to behave differently towards our patient if they have an altered level of consciousness? Are we allowed to be unloving to them even if they caused their own problems? May we not care about them if they don't care about themselves? Are we permitted to be angry with them?

No! No! No! No!

Our patient is *our patient* no matter how they ended up as our patient. Whatever they may have done before we meet them is almost irrelevant (except for those legal exceptions, e.g., suicidal/homicidal intent, abuse, etc.). The expression, "Love is Blind" definitely applies to us.

Furthermore, caring for patients offers us challenges; being challenged is good for us. However, a patient care task is never a contest. Winning a contest becomes the goal in itself. Therefore, in a contest, we lose sight of the real goal. (The real goal is always good patient care.) Nurse Macomber and Dr. Wilson both lost sight of the *real* goal (helping Ms. Zingle by raising her blood sugar), while they attacked the artificial goal (establishing an IV).

**Where's the Compassion?** Attending to a patient with an altered level of consciousness is very difficult. Although we may not be able to expect coherent answers to our questions, we still need to attend carefully to all the cues they give us. This type of attention comes with experience.

However, just because we may not hear silent cries for help, does not mean we cannot be empathetic. We should always be able to feel our patient's pain—especially pain that *we* cause from our interventions.

Nurse Macomber is a good nurse, and she loves her patients. However, while she cared for Ms. Zingle, she actually lost sight of Ms. Zingle. She lost the big picture. She saw only veins. She could not empathize with veins.

She did minister to veins, however. She ministered way too much to veins. She lost her chance to minister to Ms. Zingle.

Dr. Wilson was even worse. He had the decision-making power to order the glucagon right away. Instead, he, too, chose to minister to Ms. Zingle's veins, not to Ms. Zingle. (This is ridiculous, of course, since what *doctor* could possibly hope to start an IV on a patient that a nurse and a paramedic could not get!?)

**Where's the Respect?** Nurse Macomber and her team did not show much courtesy. They did not say, "Please hold still…" nor "Thanks for not moving…" nor "May I try an IV here?" These courtesies may seem silly with an obtunded patient; however, politeness reminds us that we are dealing with a person, not just some veins. Polite words re-focus our attention back onto *the person*. Polite, respectful words would not have taken Nurse Macomber any more time, but they may have helped stop the useless sticks sooner.

Where's the dignity in being stuck with needles a dozen times?

Of course, validating Ms. Zingle and Latesha Zingle would have been very important. Latesha deserves praise for treating her mother at home, and praise for knowing when to call paramedics. Once Ms. Zingle feels better, this visit is a perfect opportunity for face-saving and honest discussions about blood sugar control as well.

**Where's the Humility?** We all have skills. We should be proud of our skills, especially when we use those skills to help people. However, we must always be careful that we use our skills for our *patient's* sake, not for our sake. Nurse Macomber is very skilled at starting IV lines. She is also skilled at teaching students how to start IV lines. However, these skills must always be used to benefit patients, not just because she has those skills.

The proud caregiver will never admit defeat, and try and try to complete a perfect job on a patient. A humble caregiver will admit their limitations early, and seek help with a patient. A proud caregiver has their reputation at stake all the time. A humble caregiver has what's best *for their patient* as a focus all the time.

Ms. Zingle would probably not object to having student nurses start IVs on her. However, she would object to wagering on her.

It is not uncommon for caregivers to try and guess a patient's lab value. We artfully make estimates of an intoxicated patient's blood alcohol level, or on a diabetic ketoacidosis patient's blood sugar, or on a code patient's arterial pH. While our estimations are derived from our clinical experience, and have utility in patient care, *betting* and *competing* on our guesses detracts from the seriousness of the data we are guessing. No harm comes to our patients from these bets, yet harm is done. The harm is to our *perspective* of our patients, that is, how we regard our patients. Clinical care is never affected, yet we, the wagering caregivers, are harmed, by allowing our love and attention to be diverted and muddied.

Nurse Macomber and her team should have been saying, "I'm sorry" a lot. Not only does Ms. Zingle deserve apologies, but also apologizing would raise the team's awareness of what they were doing to her. After hearing several apologies, Nurse Macomber would be more likely to stop and question the merits of further attempts at IV access.

## Do the Right Thing

How would we best care for Ms. Zingle? Clearly, she needs care ... her blood sugar is dangerously low, and she is obtunded. What is the right thing to do?

Obviously, Dr. Wilson should have noted how difficult an IV might be ... even the paramedics did not start one. He could have ordered glucagon right away, and prevented the whole fiasco. However, his clinical decision was that the patient needed an IV.

If we were Nurse Macomber, we would have modeled for the team of students loving patient care. We would say, "Hi, Ms. Zingle, how are you? ... it seems your blood sugar is a little low today. Have you ever had an IV before? What's the best place for you?" We may or may not get an answer. Then, we'd say, "Looks like this might take a few tries.... Please let us try at least three times, and then if we can't get one, we'll tell the doctor."

The three strikes rule is a good one; personally, I usually use the two strikes rule on myself, for lumbar punctures, central lines, etc. We all must decide our own limits. These limits are important, since there are side effects to everything we do, and limiting patients' exposures to potential side effects is an important balance in healthcare.

No matter what we decide on attempting IV access, we would be empathetic, polite and gracious to Ms. Zingle.

Once we got Ms. Zingle's sugar up again, either by glucagon or IV dextrose, we would praise Ms. Zingle and Latesha for checking the dextrostick and giving the sugar-orange juice at home. This compliment would open the door for us to discuss diabetes and blood sugar regulation in general, as well as obesity and diet. We may need to refer Ms. Zingle to diabetic refresher classes, but we would do so because we care about her, not just because we have some protocol for the referral.

Further, discussing this event would have allowed Ms. Zingle to talk about her attempts at weight loss. Once that subject is opened, we could have praised her for her desire to lose weight, and perhaps referred her to a specialist in weight control, or a bariatric surgeon.[5]

## Practice Makes Perfect

Pick one of your patients that you least care for ... someone with whom you have a poor relationship and with whom you never got along. Then, tell your co-workers that you love that patient. Tell everyone you run into, especially co-workers who might know of your disdain, that this patient is a wonderful person. This patient handles their difficult life very well. This patient deserves praise and honors for enduring their affliction so well. Really lay it on.

Once you have told everyone how much you admire this patient, stop. Do you now admire them? Have your praises and compliments led to an epiphany? Do you love them?

Talking nicely about someone does not *make* you like them. However, it will induce a little cognitive dissonance in you. And, you might just find yourself loving your patient. In any event, you will gain insights into your patient's life that you might not otherwise have found.

## Give a Gift

Give a gift of an apology. "I am sorry you have to go through this…" or "I am sorry to meet you under these circumstances…" or "I am sorry to be causing you discomfort…" or " I am sorry you cannot understand what I am telling you…." True sorrow brims with compassion and kindness and humility. While there is no real depression or pain or sadness for us, we do help our patients with their burden. Just a little bit.

---

[5] Bariatric: Weight control surgeon, e.g., those who do laproscopic gastric banding or gastric bypass procedures.

CHAPTER

# 17

# *Ms. Horton's Story*

*M*s. Horton sat in the cold exam room, naked, except for the paper gown. She is waiting for the nurse practitioner. She is filled with a mixture of concern and excitement.

She is concerned about her symptoms. Ms. Horton came in today because she was having burning with urination and mild ache in her pelvis. She thought it might be a bladder infection, but she was not sure. Although she is fifty-seven years old, she has never had a bladder infection before.

Ms. Horton is excited about meeting the new Nurse Practitioner, Ms. Klodd. She was pleased that she got a clinic appointment to see Ms. Klodd today, and she was glad she did not have to go to the Urgent Care.

Although not a caregiver herself, Ms. Horton has worked in hospitals for many years. Her current role is Executive Director of Community Affairs, and she is involved in the local nursing school. She is bored with the arrogance of doctors, and she feels strongly that nurses need a more aggressive role in health care.

However, some of Ms. Horton's excitement has evaporated. Her excitement has been losing ground to her worries. So far, she has given a urine specimen and had her blood pressure and temperature checked. And filled out some paperwork. That's all. That was an hour and a half ago.

No one has been back in to her room to explain the delays.

To fill the time, she found herself rehearsing her opening greeting for when she meets Ms. Klodd. She rehearsed and edited the details of her symptoms over and over, wanting to include all the facts. Facts like her favorite aunt recently died of bladder cancer. Ms. Horton did not know if she could have bladder cancer, too.

"Does bladder cancer run in families?" she planned to ask.

"Are my symptoms normal for someone my age?"

"Do these symptoms have something to do with my problems with sex lately?"

Mrs. Horton had hoped for a less *clinical* setting in which to meet the new Nurse Practitioner, but she didn't mind being one of Ms. Klodd's first patients. "The cook's gotta taste the stew," she told herself.

Ms. Horton organized and re-organized the long lists of details she wanted to discuss with Ms. Klodd. She tried to maintain her enthusiasm about this new caregiver, even while she reviewed her list of concerns. She was also rehearsing how best to talk about her strong support for advanced practice nursing.

Finally, in burst Nurse Practitioner Klodd. She squinted at her clipboard as she spoke. In fact, Nurse Practitioner Klodd never took her eyes off of the clipboard.

"Hi … uh … Ms. Horton, I won't have time for your full intake with a last minute visit like this … so you're having problems with your pee, looks like a U.T.I.,[1] no big deal we'll

---

[1] UTI: Urinary tract infection, ie, infection of the urethra, bladder, ureter(s), or kidney(s).

get you a course of antibiotics and that should clear things up in no time. Probably just a gram negative enteric[2] snuck in the wrong hole, if you know what I mean. Heh, heh. If you are not better in a week or so, give us a call. Great to meet you. Bye."

And she was gone. No time for questions, no physical exam, no acknowledgment of Ms. Horton at all, really.

Ms. Horton sat there, stunned. She felt violated. She felt neglected. She felt even *worse* than before. This punched-in-the-gut feeling prevented her from organizing her thoughts enough to say anything on her way out.

The clinic nurse soon came in and hurried Ms. Horton along, giving her the prescription and pointing her towards the checkout desk. The nurse began to ready the room for the next patient even before Ms. Horton was out the door.

Ms. Horton left the nurse practitioner's office, almost in a daze. She wanted to cry, unsure of where to turn next. She went home and sat in her favorite chair. She stared out the window, sipping tea. She sat for a long time.

## Where's the Love?

"What love?" we may ask.

Now let's give the office team a break, here. Ms. Horton did, after all, make a last-minute appointment. She did have a U.T.I., which was appropriately treated with the antibiotics. And she should get better.

So why does she leave feeling worse than when she went in?

Why? Because *her illness* was all that got treated, that's why! Ms. Horton *was* a UTI, and nothing more.

---

[2] Gram negative enteric: A general class of bacteria that normally live in our large intestines. They turn pink color on Gram staining. These bacteria can cause severe infection if they contaminate any other part of our body.

Her "chief complaint" was treated, but *Ms. Horton* was ignored. She had none of her questions answered, no justification for the paper gown, no apologies for her wait. She left with all her fears and worries intact.

She will never return to this office. She will convince all of her friends to never return as well.

Ms. Horton's visit was a catastrophe.

**Where's the Compassion?** Nurse Practitioner Klodd has made the most fundamental mistake a caregiver can make. She assumed she knew what her patient wanted and needed. She assumed without asking. She assumed that Ms. Horton wanted antibiotics for a UTI. She assumed a lot about Ms. Horton. And she was wrong.

We have all heard the old saying about assuming ("When we '**assume**,' we make an '**ass**' out of '**u**' and '**me**.'") Nurse Practitioner Klodd sure did assume. A lot.

It is not that Nurse Practitioner Klodd was not empathic. She had some empathy… empathy for a UTI. She never gave *Ms. Horton* a chance to describe her worries. Ms. Klodd never asked if there was anything *else* about which she needed to be empathic!

Ms. Klodd never ministered to Ms. Horton, because Ms. Klodd did not feel that Ms. Horton's initial complaint (burning with urination) needed much support or comforting. Although she reviewed Ms. Horton's checklist, Ms. Klodd decided to wait until the next visit, when the clinic was not too busy, to discuss the points Ms. Horton had listed. However, that "next visit" will never come.

My biggest concern with Ms. Klodd was her lack of attention to her patient. She never let Ms. Horton speak! Even while she sat in front of her, Ms. Klodd ignored Ms. Horton! (Did you feel like taking Ms. Klodd's head and directing it so she had to look into Ms. Horton's eyes? Yes? Good!) Not listening, not determining the reasons behind a patient's complaint, is very common.

While her UTI was treated, Ms. Horton, the person, was ignored.

**Where's the Respect?** Certainly, we might say, Ms. Horton was treated with respect. Everyone was pleasant and courteous. Everyone smiled. Everyone in the office went through the motions of their patient-satisfaction-training program properly (even if they *were* a little behind schedule with Ms. Horton). Even Ms. Klodd greeted her patient warmly.

So why was Ms. Horton so unhappy with her visit?

Because empty respect does not warm any hearts. Ms. Horton was not treated as a guest. She was regarded as a symptom, an illness, a diagnosis. She *was* a U.T.I.

No one was *interested* in Ms. Horton. No one acknowledged her worries or her fears. No one tried to validate her concerns. No one explained the delays. Aside from the routine intake checklist, no one asked her *any* personal questions.

Wait a minute, we might say. Isn't Ms. Horton being a little unrealistic, wanting time for questions and reassurances, which could be addressed at a regularly scheduled office visit, where a full fifteen minutes is allotted for all that sort of chitchat?

Or perhaps there's a communication problem. Shouldn't Ms. Horton have been more assertive to get her needs met?

No! It is our job to be absolutely certain that we dignify our patients with an acknowledgment of their concerns. Just as there are no stupid questions, there are no stupid concerns! Every single worry, from, "Is this lump a cancer?" to "When should I use the call light?" is valid, relevant and important.

**Where's the Humility?** What is up with Nurse Practitioner Klodd anyway? She's late. She doesn't apologize. She doesn't thank Ms. Horton for her patience. She makes a crude joke ("a gram negative enteric snuck in the wrong hole") using medical jargon (and she doesn't even translate the joke!).

I suspect Nurse Practitioner Klodd is too busy. In her zeal to accomplish all her little tasks, she forgets about the people attached to those tasks. Ms. Klodd is too busy to notice.

Ms. Klodd has no time for translations, no time for admirations, no time for graciousness. Nurse Practitioner Klodd is too busy to even see the patient she is seeing!

## Do the Right Thing

We all get busy. Sometimes crazy busy. Sometimes too busy.

When I am at work, I know I am *too* busy if I forget the art of agape. When I forget to listen to someone's story, I am too busy. When I forget to say my patient's name, I am too busy. When I forget to translate what is going on, I am too busy.

Patients understand when we are very busy. They know our job can be stressful. I have never had a patient get upset and demand to talk to me if they knew I was caring for someone who is sicker than they are.

However, it gets tiresome for patients when they are always ignored, always made to wait, or their "little things" are passed onto the next caregiver.

What is the best way to care for patients when we are busy?

First, explain. Our patients will understand being ignored if they agree it is for a good reason. When we are running between critical patients, other patients understand delays. If we are sitting around the nurse's station, chatting away, they are less understanding.

Second, ask the patient for their help. Our patients all want to be helpful. Everyone would like to help another person in need. We could say, "Please help me. I need your patience while I tend to this very sick person right over here. I will be with you soon." Waiting patiently is easy when someone believes it is for the benefit of a sick or needy person.

The only help we are asking for is patience. This is easy to give. And, patients are very flattered that we bother to ask for that help, instead of us just assuming they will help us.

Third, say *when* or *how* the person who is waiting will be cared for. Our patients do not expect us to do everything, but they do expect that their questions or concerns will be addressed. Sooner or later. By someone.

For example, Ms. Klodd could have said to Ms. Horton, "Hi, I am sorry we are behind schedule, we had a critically ill patient in here earlier.... I need your help. Please be patient with us. Although it looks like you have a bladder infection, I understand that you have several concerns. Would you rather come back tomorrow or at another time to talk about them, or shall I get someone else to help sooner?"

This sort of interaction would take no more time, and would be vastly more rewarding for Ms. Horton.

What else can we learn from Ms. Klodd?

Everyone has a story to tell. As we discussed in Chapter 4, patients need to tell their story. It may be long and complex, or just one sentence, but if we do not listen to their story, they will be unfulfilled. They will be unhappy. Their visit is not complete. They may leave us and may never return.

I have cared for many, many patients who quit their primary caregiver because the caregiver did not listen to their story. Every patient has a perception of what is important or relevant. Sure, sometimes our patients are way off the mark, and need to be re-directed to more relevant material, but we absolutely must listen to them first, at least a little bit, to determine what *is* important to them.

Listen. Listen attentively. Listen with interest. And please, we must act like we care! For at least ten seconds of every patient visit, I put down my chart, put down my pen, and I make eye contact. Then, I listen. Sometimes, I ask my patients to look at me, so they can see that I have my full attention directed towards them. Once we get past the point where they *know* I am listening, I can do other things. I can then check their IV, take notes, or feel their pulse. And it's okay. They still have my attention.

Everyone has a story to tell. Some stories are one or two words (e.g., "It hurts!"). Some stories could fill books. All stories need a little bit of our time.

If Nurse Practitioner Klodd listened to Ms. Horton's story, she would have discovered that Ms. Horton was influential at the nursing school, and that Ms. Horton could help Ms. Klodd get on the faculty there, as she so wanted to do.

My other big concern with Ms. Horton's care was the dismissive way she was regarded. She was her illness. Ms. Horton is a bright, energetic person. Perhaps there is not time to get to know her. However, ignoring her for an hour-and-a-half just because her complaint is not serious is bad. Real bad.

No one is their illness!

Please, let's all try to get out of the habit of referring to a patient by their diagnosis. Not only does it dehumanize our patients, it shows everyone we are lazy and uncaring. "The patient with dysuria[3] in room 2," is just as easy to say as "The burning with urination in room 2," and is so much nicer.

Every inch we creep *away from* the people for whom we care is an inch closer to our burnout, to our cynicism, and our own unhappiness.

---

[3] Dysuria: Difficulty or pain with urination. This symptom commonly implies a possible urinary tract infection.

## Practice Makes Perfect

Let someone know that you are interested in what they have to say. Really interested. Enthralled. Captivated. Do whatever it takes until this person is absolutely certain that you are intensely interested in them. Look at them. Nod. Smile. Encourage them to talk more. Have "open" body language (arms not crossed, with your body directed at the person ... even use encouraging hand gestures).

You can practice this with people outside work. When you are skilled, and you can quickly show your keen interest in someone, practice it at work. You will surprise people.

Your sincere interest in them will be very validating. Your interest will be very therapeutic.

All too often, people assume they will be ignored. Our patients often suspect that only their ill body-part will get any attention. When you express your deep interest in them, you will be amazed at the gifts that *you* will receive.

## Give a Gift

Give a gift of politeness. Whenever you speak, make sure that you say, "please," or "thank you," or "would you mind?" Enter and leave every patient's room, and every person's company, with a greeting or a salutation.

There are many ways to be polite. Pick a few that work for you, and be polite!

# Mr. Annuge's Patient Smile

Steven Annuge (pronounced ah-NU-gay) was very excited. He was going to the dentist for the first time.

At age twenty-nine, Mr. Annuge had never felt any reason to go to a dentist before. He seldom brushed his teeth (although he often smiles). Some of the people where he lives seldom brush their teeth, too. No one ever told him to do it, so he doesn't. However, his regular doctor told him his mouth looked raw, and he should have his teeth cleaned. When Mr. Annuge found out he would get a free toothbrush if he had his teeth cleaned, he was very excited.

Mr. Annuge is developmentally disabled.

He arrived at the dentist's office with his eyes wide and feeling a little nervous. His group home supervisor came in with him to help with the paperwork, and give his medical history. However, the supervisor had to leave. His supervisor said he'd be back in an hour or so.

Mr. Annuge waited quietly. The new smells and sounds were a little disorienting. However, he looked at some magazines. Just as he was told. He stayed seated. Just as he was told. He waited patiently. Just as he was told.

Ms. Gloria Marten is a dental hygienist, and she is *very* hygienic. She keeps a tidy workspace. She is efficient. She is neat, clean and proper. And, she expects the same from her patients.

Her work area is decorated with her plaques, awards and letters of commendation. She is the president of the state hygienist association. She has been cleaning teeth for over ten years. She works in a prestigious dental practice in a large suburban office.

Ms. Marten stepped into the waiting room to call her new patient.

"Mr. Annuge?"

When Mr. Annuge proudly stood up, Ms. Marten recoiled. She was mortified. She stared in revulsion at his unshaven face and at the tiny catsup stains from breakfast on his shirtfront, his best shirt, which was buttoned all the way to the top. She wrinkled her face when she noticed just a hint of body odor. She did not return his wide smile or his friendly "Hi!" She did not even try to hide the look of …disgust… on her face as she ushered him down the hall. Mr. Annuge cautiously moved towards the exam room.

"OK, uh, Steve, let's see here, it says your last appointment was … when was your last cleaning, uh, Steve?"

He was eyeing the instruments suspiciously.

"Not ever," he said.

"Never?" Ms. Marten shrieked, with annoyance. "You have *never* had your teeth cleaned?" Annoyance and disbelief. "Not *once* in your life have you been to the dentist to have your teeth cleaned?" Annoyance and disbelief and disgust.

"Nope." Mr. Annuge smiled, and Ms. Marten actually stepped back, a look of fear on her face, as she noticed how … unclean … his teeth were.

"Excuse me." Ms. Marten left the room.

Mr. Annuge sensed he might have done something wrong, but he could not think what it might have been. He has done everything he was told to do.

Mr. Annuge could hear Ms. Marten complaining in the next room. "…He's a retardate … never cleaned … nasty…" He was not sure if she was talking about him, but he knew she was upset.

A few minutes later Ms. Marten returned. She had placed a surgical mask over her face, but even the mask could not hide the revulsion in her eyes. She said, "Open wide."

Slowly, Mr. Annuge did as he was told.

The plaque on his teeth was thick and hard. His gingivae were red and swollen. Ms. Marten shook her head. She moved toward her sink, but then mumbled, "I'm not even gonna bother washing my hands." She snapped on some gloves.

Reluctantly, Ms. Marten went to work.

The whole time she was cleaning, she never stopped criticizing Mr. Annuge.

"I can't believe you've never brushed your teeth!"

"Oh … this is the worst mouth I have ever seen!"

"Don't you even know what floss *is*?"

"Yuck!"

"This is so gross!"

Mr. Annuge knew she was unhappy, and he knew it was because of him. He tried to talk to her several times, but she would just make him rinse or open wide again. When he flinched in pain, she would chide, "Hold still!" or "This is hard enough without you moving!" or "Oh! Stop!"

Sometimes she just grabbed his chin and roughly straightened him back into position.

She used the sickle scaler and the universal curette and the Gracey curette.[1] She used all the tools she had. She would

---

[1] Professional instruments for cleaning teeth and the surrounding tissues.

sometimes cough, and wince, or turn her head away. Mr. Annuge felt he was being scolded, but he did not know what he had done wrong.

The hostile look in her eyes said more than her bitter words.

Sometimes Ms. Marten would leave the room and complain to her dentist. Though her words were muffled, Mr. Annuge could hear anger.

Finally, after forty-five minutes, she was finished.

Mr. Annuge felt ashamed, but he was not exactly sure why. He rinsed one last time, and she unclipped his bib and lifted the arm of the chair. She stepped back instead of helping her patient out of the chair. She took his paperwork to the front desk, expecting him to follow.

He stood by the chair and waited.

When Ms. Marten returned to the room and Mr. Annuge was still standing there, she thought she was going to have a problem. She looked at him fearfully.

"It's time for you to go. Now. Out to the front." Stepping out of the doorway, she pointed down the hallway.

"What about my toothbrush?" asked Mr. Annuge.

"What? What for? Oh well, I guess so." She opened her cabinet and grabbed a small plastic bag. The bag had a smiling tooth on it. It contained a toothbrush, floss and a pamphlet on dental care.

She thrust it at Mr. Annuge. "Here. Take it. Now go."

Mr. Annuge smiled, accepting the gift. He looked inside the bag.

"Thank you very much," he said as he left the exam room. He slowly made his way out front.

### Where's the Love?

How was Ms. Annuge's care? Ms. Marten *did* clean his teeth. She did a good job of it, too. He will have less decay and tooth loss now. And besides, we all have patients we'd rather not care for, so what's the big deal?

The big deal is that Ms. Marten's behavior was atrocious. We could criticize Ms. Marten many times, in many ways, for the shameful way she took care of Mr. Annuge. Let's discuss a few of them.

**Where's the Compassion?** Mr. Annuge does not need pity. He is an adult. He does, however, need some comforting and reassurance.

Ms. Marten should have immediately sensed Mr. Annuge's apprehension. Instead of being disgusted by the fact that this was his first time to the hygienist's, she should have empathized with his anxiety at a first visit.

If anyone needs ministering, it's a first-time dental patient. As with any health care facility, a dental office is full of strange smells, sounds and lights. It's very anxiety-provoking. Mr. Annuge is very trusting. Although he is concerned, he is obedient. He does what he is told. He trusts Ms. Marten completely.

If she had attended to Mr. Annuge *as a person*, and not attended to his flaws, she would have noticed his fears. She does not even *pretend* to care about his anxiety. She chooses to *not* read her patient. She instead focuses on Mr. Annuge's imperfections.

She did not even try to comfort him. She capitalized on *his* trust, using it as a way to minimize her interaction with her patient. She saw his trust as a license to avoid ministering to him. Despite his trust, Mr. Annuge was quite anxious, and he could have used a little comforting.

Perhaps the saddest aspect of Ms. Marten's care was her attention to Mr. Annuge's imperfections. If she had attended to him, *as a person,* his teeth, his clothing, his *flaws*, would have been in the background, where they belong.

**Where's the Respect?** The only thing worse than ignoring a patient is speaking rudely about them. To their face.

Over and over again. Ms. Marten's incessant picking, sniping and criticizing is one of the rudest things a patient can hear. It is so far from love, it should never happen.

She doesn't even try to allow him to save face. She doesn't return his warm greeting. She doesn't call him "Mr." She doesn't even wash her hands! Would she behave like that with a guest in her home?

While it's true a dentist's office is a difficult place to have a conversation, Ms. Marten did not even *try* to talk with her patient.

On one level, Ms. Marten *was* honest. She did not even try to hide her disgust. However, we must regard this type of honesty as destructive to patient care. This type of display, which is almost an emotional outburst, is never beneficial to patient care. It's disrespectful and self-serving.

Any first-time patient needs to be complimented and praised for coming in. Over and over again.

**Where's the Humility?** It is shocking that a healthcare professional would not *teach* a patient preventive care. Mr. Annuge never had anyone teach him how to brush, so he rarely does it. Ms. Marten assumed he didn't brush his teeth because he *would* not do it. However, Mr. Annuge does not brush his teeth because he does not know *how* to brush his teeth. It's simply a skills deficit: Mr. Annuge was never properly taught how to brush his teeth.

Ms. Marten was so absorbed in her own disgust that she failed to care for *him*. This is a common and fundamental problem at times: We are so busy reacting *to* the patient that we forget to care *for* them. Our own feelings sometimes are so overwhelming that we forget to get past those feelings. We become self-absorbed. We forget our patient.

It's always important to notice our reactions to people. However, our reactions should never be the *focus* of our attention. Our reactions, even if they are negative, are never an excuse for rude, verbal assaults on our patients.

Ms. Marten had forty-five minutes to teach Mr. Annuge about his teeth. She never explained what she was doing, why she was doing it, how the plaque develops or why plaque is bad. She never explained to Mr. Annuge how to prevent plaque buildup, how to brush, how to floss or how to care for his teeth. Instead, Ms. Marten shared only her self-centered reactions.

Had Ms. Marten admired Mr. Annuge for his courage, she might have learned something about him, his hobbies or his pastimes. She might have learned that he shares a common interest with her father: trading baseball cards.

## Do the Right Thing

Have you ever been "grossed out" on the job? If not, don't worry. It will happen sooner or later. I have cared for patients who had intestinal worms squirming out of their anus. I've met patients who had maggots that filled their leg wound. I once cared for a man who had roaches scurrying out of his sleeves. Each of these patients needed my care. Each one was glad I did not make a big deal out of their situation.

How can we care for a patient when their physical ailment makes us totally grossed out or disgusted or horrified? The answer is obvious: Don't get grossed out.

No matter how nasty or repulsive a patient may seem on initial evaluation, that *person* must be regarded independently of whatever is bothering *us*. That is to say, a patient should never gross us out, even though their circumstances may be disgusting. *Mr. Annuge* should not horrify anyone, but his *teeth* might.

One of the reasons healthcare workers go through extensive training and schooling and orientation is to *desensitize* us. Desensitize means to reduce our reaction to something by seeing it over and over. The first day in gross anatomy, some medical student will inevitably suffer a syncopal episode. On their first day in the operating room, a student usually has to be helped into a chair. But later in the experience, it's all very relaxed. No one is getting sick or falling out. Most of us were once squeamish at the sight of blood or feces or sputum or vomitus, but now, that stuff is no big deal. We've gotten desensitized.

One caveat here is that we must be very careful that we don't become desensitized to other people's pain and suffering. That's the whole idea of doing our jobs with agape: To be more sensitive to people, even though our training may have desensitized us to their physical ailment.

Once we can look past a patient's disturbing physical problem, we can begin to see the patient, and we can begin to care for that patient. No matter how nasty or offensive their clothing, their hygiene, or their surroundings may be, we must always look past that stuff and see *the patient*.

Remember, when we focus on the grotesque things, we are actually focusing on our selves and our reactions, not on our patient. Our focus should always be on our patient.

Needless to say, when we first meet Mr. Annuge, we'd return his salutation with an equally warm greeting and introduction. We'd look past his slightly "unkempt" exterior, and notice his warm smile. We'd smile back.

We'd notice his hesitation. We'd see he is apprehensive. Our words would be soft and comforting. For example, "So, you've never been here before, have you? Well, it's a little bit funny at first, but don't worry, we'll take good care of you." Or perhaps, "First time? It's a great place, once you get used to it. Can I answer any questions for you?" By devoting more of our time to his *feelings* and less time to *our reactions* to him, we'd offer Mr. Annuge a very pleasant visit.

Of course, we'd address him as Mr. Annuge. Remember, some people are almost never addressed with Mr. or Ms. When we offer this respectful title, we honor them.

No matter what, we would never express our disgust or disdain. We would offer face-saving ways to express our concern about his teeth. For example, we might say, "I see you have quite a bit of plaque on your teeth. Before you leave, let's make sure we review good brushing. It'll make your mouth more comfortable." We can never shame or embarrass our patients.

Our teaching must be directed at a level appropriate for Mr. Annuge. If we can't guess his developmental level, that is, if we do not know how complex our language should be, then it may be helpful to have his group home supervisor be with us before we do any teaching. Mr. Annuge's developmental disability does not mean we treat him any differently, it just means we should be sure that what we say is appropriate and understood. The burden is on *us* to be understood, not on our patients to understand.

## Practice Makes Perfect

Notice your reactions. Notice how you react to another person. Notice your judgments and your opinions when you see, hear, and smell your patient. Notice how your attention is drawn to their peculiarity. Do you stare at their birthmark, their scar, or their amputation? Do you notice their speech or their dandruff? How do you feel when you notice these things?

Your reactions may have some clinical importance. For example, does this patient make you sad? If so, are they clinically depressed? Does this patient smell of ketones, making you think of dehydration or DKA?[2] Do you smell urine, raising your suspicion of neglect?

Don't ignore your reactions. Instead, recognize that those reactions to your patient are your personal property. They are your possessions. As your possessions, they should not be shared, except with the goal of helping your patient.

Once you notice your own observations, put those observations aside. Put your reactions up on a shelf somewhere, and then notice your patient. When you separate your reactions from the person in front of you, you will have crossed a great line in your clinical practice. You will love your patient.

### Give a Gift

Give a nice, warm handshake. Not just the usual limp washrag that slides across their fingers, but a deep, meaningful handshake. Try two hands, or a long one, or a good firm squeeze. Or better yet, shake hands and keep holding your patient's fingers or hand until they break contact. This contact is especially important for a patient you'd rather not touch. When you shake their hand, you will communicate your love to them.

---

[2] DKA: Diabetic keto-acidosis.

# part III

# The Art of Agape

*I* hope you agree that agape is crucial for our care of patients. In this section, I will review a few of the papers that scientifically analyze how and why agape-type behaviors make good clinical sense. There are many good, statistically accurate studies that address the topics we have discussed; we will review a selected sample.

The data, which support using agape in our clinical life, are everywhere. Although physicians publish many of the papers cited, the nursing literature is particularly advanced in this area.

Unlike most physician-authored papers, the nurse-authored papers usually include theoretical underpinnings and philosophical discussions. I feel that these discussions reflect an important difference between physicians and nurses: Nurses often recognize the *interpersonal interaction* as a crucial component of healthcare. Unfortunately, as healthcare technology becomes more advanced, nurses, too, risk losing that close, personal contact with their patients.

The literature on these topics is amorphous. Agape-quality interactions are subsumed under various umbrellas such as "compassionate care," "respectful care," "professionalism," "patient-centered medicine," and "biopsychosocial medicine."

As alluded to in Part I, agape is good for patients and good for caregivers. For patients, the benefits fall in two categories. First, patients enjoy improved outcomes with any given healthcare intervention. This occurs mainly when we *teach* our patients about what's going on. Second, patients are happier, and more satisfied, with their care. This improvement in patient satisfaction reflects a variety of factors.

Caregivers who approach their patients with agape find two key advantages. First, we have higher job satisfaction. Second, agape-trained caregivers suffer fewer lawsuits. There are many papers that discuss reducing litigation risk by being nicer.

Later in this section, we will discuss teaching. Teaching is perhaps the final common denominator of agape. When we teach our patients, teach them anything, we involve all the component parts of agape.

Finally, we will discuss personality and a little of the philosophy of agape.

# *Agape:*
# *It's Good for Everyone!*
## A *Review of the Related Literature*

In this chapter, we will examine some of the published literature that supports and endorses the art of agape. Most of these studies investigate the *style* and *content* of patient-caregiver communication.

First, we will review articles that discuss patients' health benefits, when we behave with agape. Then we will review the topic of patient satisfaction and agape. Finally, we will discuss *us*, and how agape is associated with higher caregiver satisfaction and reduced medical malpractice risks.

I do not attempt to review all the articles that could be considered supportive of the tenets of agape. Instead, I have chosen several representative and/or pertinent studies. In my searches, I noticed several groups of authors that consistently publish high quality works. I will mention those groups as we discuss their papers.

### Agape: It's Good for Our Patients

Patients get better faster, and stay better longer, when treated with agape

The most relevant question we might ask is, "Do patients get better faster when we, the caregivers, treat them with love?" The answer is a resounding, "YES!" There are several excellent studies that investigate this. (None of these studies uses the word "agape" or "love." However, the papers usually discuss "compassion" or "respect" or some other concept that is subsumed under agape. Let us keep a broad definition of agape.)

In the last several decades, there has been an increased recognition of the fact that happy patients, or at least satisfied patients, are healthier, and stay healthier longer.

Paul Little and colleagues (2001), in Great Britain, have researched this topic as patient centeredness. In one study, they analyzed interactions involving 865 patients! The authors concluded that:

"If doctors do not provide a positive, patient-centered approach, patients will be less satisfied, less enabled, and may have greater symptom burden and use more health service resources."

After analyzing their data, they feel that patient-centered care (which embodies many of the components of agape) allows for more satisfied patients, with fewer symptoms, who seek health care less often!

And nurses, do not fret. Although these authors did not mention other caregivers specifically, they did determine that being "given a prescription" or "not being given a prescription" was *not* associated with higher satisfaction scores, while communication and partnership *were* associated with higher satisfaction scores. Nurses often communicate and partner better than doctors!

Thus, this research paper suggests that we need to recognize how our actions (they cite, specifically, communication and partnership, personal relationship, health promotion, positive approach to diagnosis and prognosis, and interest in the effect on life ... all of which imply acting with agape) can actually cause our patients to have fewer symptoms!

In a related paper, a brilliant study from Canada, the researchers investigated factors that influenced frequent return visits to emergency departments in several hospitals in Toronto (Redelmeier et al, 1995). The subjects were homeless persons who regularly visit ERs for vague and non-medical reasons. The researchers randomized these frequently revisiting patients to one of two groups: Compassionate care plus standard medical care, or just standard medical care. Compassionate care consisted of a volunteer, student or other person who just sat with the patient, chatted with them, or got water or blankets or other things for them.

The compassionate care group returned less frequently to the hospitals! It seems that once their need for interpersonal contact was fulfilled, these patients sought fewer medical visits. This is a great study! It debunks the idea that being nice to people will reinforce their hospital-visiting behaviors and encourage them to return more often! Compassionate care *reduces* the frequency with which this population visits hospitals.

In an older paper, by Bartlett et al (1984), the researchers investigated how caregiver communication skills impacted patient satisfaction, as well as patient adherence to their medication regimen. They worked with mostly chronic medical patients.

These researchers found that, "medication adherence was influenced by patient satisfaction with the visit and recall of the regimen, which in turn were determined by the quality of the physician's interpersonal skills and by the amount of patient teaching … interpersonal skills were found to be a more important determinant of patient outcome than teaching."

Their "interpersonal skills" are essentially behaving with the art of agape. Again, non-physicians should not be put off by these data: Patient teaching and other patient guidance programs are more commonly given by nurses, dieticians, physical therapists, etc. Furthermore, in this study, patients' highest satisfaction rating was for the category "treated with respect." One does not have to be a physician in order to treat someone with respect.

They hypothesized that "demonstration of empathy, concern, and respect lessens the patient's anxiety and thus permits better comprehension of instructions and advice." Whatever the mechanism, agape helps patients manage their chronic medical problems.

In the book *Patient Centered Medicine*, by Moira Stewart et al (1995), the authors review the published literature on caregiver behaviors and patient outcome. Ms. Stewart feels that sixteen of twenty-one studies demonstrate a positive effect on patients when the caregivers applied tenets of patient centered medicine. Since much of patient centered medicine incorporates the art of agape, as we discussed, this review supports the belief that agape is good for our patients' health.

Research has pointed out a strong association between increased patient satisfaction and increased compliance and health. Bell and Krivich do a very nice review of this in their 2000 book, *How to Use Patient Satisfaction Data to Improve Healthcare Quality*. They state,

"First, patients who are satisfied are more compliant. That is, they will follow their treatment protocols more completely. Second, satisfied patients are more likely to return for follow-up visits, complete drug regimens, and in the process get well faster. Third, patient satisfaction data provide managers with useful information regarding the outcomes of care. Since satisfaction can be viewed as a proxy measure for the outcome of care, patient perceptions can point out process areas needing improvement."

Thus, patient satisfaction ratings are an indirect measure of what the patient takes home from their healthcare encounter. These authors feel that satisfaction scores reflect treatment success!

## Patient Satisfaction Increases with Agape

This concept is not difficult: When caregivers are nice, patients are happy. Some of these studies compare clinicians who have undergone training in communication skills, empathy skills or interpersonal interaction skills to clinicians who have not undergone training. Some of the studies ask patients why they were dissatisfied with their care. The more interesting studies explore patients' reactions to specific events while they were sick.

In an excellent review of the patient satisfaction literature for emergency departments (ED), Boudreaux and O'Hea (2004) analyzed fifty of the best designed and implemented research articles. Their review determined that "The predictor domain most strongly associated with global ED satisfaction ... was patient satisfaction with interpersonal interactions with ED providers [doctors and nurses]." They define "interpersonal interactions" as including expressive quality (interpersonal mannerisms and perceived humanitarian concern of the provider, or simply, bedside manner), information delivery (the amount, quality and understandability of information given to the patient during the ED visit), as well as responsiveness and availability. Improving interpersonal interactions is exactly what the art of agape is all about!

In a brilliant 2001 paper on nurse caring behaviors, Kipp reviews how implementing caring standards in an emergency department increased patient satisfaction ratings. The caring standards included most of what we call agape!

I love this! This supports what we have been discussing! And, these standards "appeared to be effective in improving staff caring behaviors and ED patient satisfaction." Patient satisfaction increases with agape!

Paramedics have been active in this field, too. Doering, in a 1998 paper, reviewed patient satisfaction assessments from patients who had been transported by ambulance. The results were incredible: Their analysis of patients' ratings placed "courtesy and politeness" as having the most impact on patient satisfaction scores, even above "level of medical care" and "response times"! The 166 respondents in this study felt that their satisfaction was most influenced by paramedics who were courteous and polite.

### Caregivers Are Happier with Agape

The literature on this topic is scarce. It seems that *our* satisfaction is not as important as patient satisfaction.

Probst et al (1997) examine both patient and physician satisfaction with an outpatient care visit. They determined that physicians were more satisfied if the patient was satisfied, *and* if the physician was comfortable. Physicians were also more satisfied with a visit if they had enough time to address the patient's problems. It may be a logical leap, but if agape increases patient satisfaction, as we discussed above, then, according to this article, agape should also increase physician satisfaction.

The internal medicine training program in Rochester, NY has as its goal, training "professionalism." In an article reviewing the training program, Markakis, Beckman, Suchman, and Frankel (2000) discuss the important points of the program. "The Path to Professionalism: Cultivating Humanistic Values and Attitudes in Residency Training" reviews the program, which includes communication skills training (which embody much of the art of agape), visiting patients at home, and a mentoring program. While this article is not a statistical research paper, the authors' enthusiasm and admiration for the teaching of professionalism leaps off the pages. Clearly, their pride at implementing and developing such a program suggests that they are very satisfied caregivers.

This group of researchers has been instrumental in advancing the science and the body of literature on improving caregiver-patient communications and interactions. They consistently publish high quality articles always worth reading.

In another non-research paper, White (1999) discusses how compassionate care has helped him survive thirty-five years as an orthopedic surgeon. His essay is light and enjoyable; the reader almost envies the joy he describes with his job. He advises caregivers to have humility, to apologize, to treat patients with respect, as well as "Educate patients, listen to them, serve them." He could (almost) have contributed to this text! He counsels us to "have some fun every day at work." He also points out that "no managed care plan, nor any bureaucracy, can extract from medical caregivers the direct immediate gratification of helping another human being." I agree. And, no matter what our job, one of the best ways we can help another human being is by behaving with agape.

A very nice article by Lipkin Jr., in the OB-GYN literature, from 1996, investigates the utility of standardized interview skills for physicians while counseling about fertility. The "skills" discussed are similar to the art of agape. The authors show that using these skills (which include overcoming barriers to communication and developing a therapeutic relationship) lead to more physician satisfaction as well as to more patient satisfaction.

Interestingly, the quality of the caregiver-patient relationship was noted to be an important part of job satisfaction for nursing assistants (in Friedman et al, 1999) and dentists (Shugars et al, 1990).

Burnout is a very real risk for us, in the caring professions. There are a huge number of articles on burnout (searching on PubMed gives over 3500 articles!) One of the factors most associated with burnout is depersonalization, also known as a lack of empathy. However, being empathic alone does not prevent burnout. In a helpful resource, *Communication Skills for Doctors*, Maguire (2000) discusses how to communicate effectively and survive emotionally. I found the discussion very helpful. The information he reviews can be applied to all caregivers. Maguire definitely feels that improving our communication skills (which I see as increasing our practice of the art of agape) will help reduce burnout.

Perhaps one of the best resources on caregiver-patient interactions I found was the nursing text, *Communications in Nursing*, by Julia W. Balzer-Riley. She grasps the human element of training (styles of interacting, boundaries, and relating well) better than most other textbooks. (She also has a nice website!) If your nursing program does not use this book, consider looking at it on your own.

### Agape Reduces Litigation Risks

Medical malpractice litigation is neither sensitive nor specific (see, e.g., the 1991 Harvard Medical Practice Study, published under Locailo et al [1991]). That means the presence or absence of negligence does not determine the likelihood of being sued. There are multiple factors involved; it is beyond our scope to review all these factors. We have already discussed several papers that address the role care-giver communication plays in reducing litigation risks. However, the impact *our behavior* has on a patient decision to file suit cannot be underestimated. Let's review more of the papers now.

"Physician-Patient Communication," a 1997 paper by Levinson, Roter, Mullooly, Dull, and Frankel, reviewed 1265 audiotapes of patient-physician conversations. The physicians were either classed as having had prior claims, i.e., litigation (at least two claims), or no claims. Primary care physicians with no claims interacted differently than primary care physicians with claims history. The no-claims physicians oriented patients more, that is, they explained what the visit would be like. They also facilitated more, that is, the no-claims physicians asked more open-ended questions and tried to get patients to explain more. Finally, the no-claims physicians showed more "warmth and friendliness," as evidenced by humor and laughing.

I definitely see agape in some of the behaviors that distinguish "no claims" from "claims" primary care physicians. They kept patients informed, they listened more (via open-ended questions), and they were warmer.

This study is unique and effective because they analyzed actual conversations. They did not use a questionnaire. This study comes from a group of caregivers who have been leaders in publishing quality, helpful literature on patient-caregiver interactions. They have developed a training program for communication skills (Levinson & Roter, 1993) and have investigated many aspects of improving the quality of caregiver interactions. I refer you, without reservation, to other articles by this team. Furthermore, the book, *Doctors Talking with Patients, Patients Talking with Doctors*, by Roter and Hall, is another detailed resource on communication.

In a straightforward and articulate discussion of this topic, Bartlett (1988) explains how "three out of four malpractice claims arise primarily from a breakdown in patient communications." Most notably, Bartlett cites "Lack of courtesy and respect" and "Inadequate handling of angry patients" as caregiver behaviors that lead to litigation. Certainly, caregivers who can practice agape, while providing good care, will decrease these risks substantially.

Virshup, Oppenberg and Coleman (1999) describe their CME course that teaches *active listening* as a means of reducing malpractice risk. This is beautiful! Active listening is a key part of agape!

In a pair of landmark studies, Hickson et al (1994) and Entman et al (1994) demonstrate that litigation is *not* related to quality of medical care and, that physicians who *are* sued are more likely to have complaints about their interpersonal care. Hickson writes: "Physicians who had never been sued were more likely to be seen by their patients as concerned, accessible and willing to communicate…. Physicians who had been sued frequently … were most likely to be seen as hurried, uninterested, and unwilling to listen and answer questions." Again, we see sparkles of agape shining from the pages of this paper. Most interesting, the authors felt that it did not matter if a physician cared about their patient; what matters more is that the physician is not seen as being "brusque and unavailable." These authors show how it does not matter what we *feel*; what matters is how we *behave*.

We have praised papers from the Beckman group in Rochester, NY previously. They, too, review malpractice cases (Beckman et al, 1994), and they conclude that "perceived lack of care" contributed to the decision to litigate in over 70% of the malpractices cases they reviewed. They cited "devaluing a patient's or family's view" as the worst offense. This sounds like the physicians who were sued failed to *validate* their patients' concerns.

A survey of physicians who have never been sued (Mangles, 1991) reveals that these physicians believe that acting with agape is important to avoid litigation. Advice such as "Respect the patient's dignity," "Listen patiently," "Be polite, no matter what," and "Be straightforward about accidents and bad results," completely support the points in this book!

Although I allow us some poetic license in interpreting these studies, I feel that the published literature supports our belief that when caregivers act with agape, everyone benefits.

**Summary: There are many published papers in which aspects of agape are shown to positively impact patients and caregivers.**

CHAPTER

## 20

# Those Who Can, Do; Those Who Love Their Patients, Teach!

*T*eaching is the purest manifestation of agape. No matter what our job may be, at some point we will care for patients who are confused or lost or unsure. When we teach them about what's going on, we show our love for them.

When we love our patients, we will teach them whatever we know. We will teach them about their metabolic processes, their diet, or how to open their milk carton. We'll teach them about their illness, their medications or what paperwork they need to bring with them each visit. We'll teach them about anything. We teach because we want them to have a good experience.

Quality teaching requires agape

### Teaching and Compassion

Teaching requires compassion. In order to know *what* we need to teach, we empathize with our patients. We understand what it feels like to have no idea what is going on. We pay attention to their reactions, to see if our teaching is helping. We smile warmly when they seem to understand.

Teaching is ministering. We teach because we care. Teaching provides reassurances that will comfort our patients long after we have left them. Often we get next to them, or touch them, to teach. Patients appreciate this. We show our patients that we are invested in them when we say, "I want to share with you…" or some other phrase using "I."

Teaching requires that we give our full attention to our audience. We must listen carefully to their concerns and confusions, so we can know what and how to teach. They will know we are focused on them by our warm eye contact.

## Teaching and Respect

Nobody wants to hear a rude teacher. Successful teaching requires us to be respectful. Patients will enjoy our instructions when we are courteous. Embarrassing medical information, shared politely and with dignity, can sometimes make a patient's visit enjoyable.

Most importantly, *there are no stupid questions!* We validate our patients when we provide face-saving answers to *all* their questions. Good teachers don't argue; they acknowledge and affirm, even when they do not agree. The *best* teachers answer the questions that are never asked.

Quality teaching is crafted specifically for each patient. We honestly assess their level of understanding before presenting any information. We explain why they are in control of their own health.

## Teaching and Humility

We must be humble for our teaching to be well received. No one wants to listen to some pompous loud-mouth. Teaching is effective when our focus is on our patient, not us.

We translate our knowledge into understandable terms. This is the hallmark or *sine qua non* of good care. Our patients leave us knowing what we have done for them, and why it was done. They understand things around them just a little bit more, and it is because of us.

As teachers, we admire their willingness to listen. We praise them for wanting to learn more, and we thank them for their attention to us. We trust that they will do the right thing.

And all this we do with grace. We apologize for those other caregivers who may not have taken the time to teach. All our advice, wisdom and instructions are offered gently and warmly, and with a sincere smile.

### Better Outcomes with Teaching

In the last chapter, we discussed research articles that show improved patient outcomes with good communication skills. The outcomes were good because the patient was *taught* about their illness, and ways to manage it.

Let's look at some similar papers.

In a brilliant review, Bodenheimer et al (2002) compare two styles of patient teaching: Patient education versus Self-management education. The latter style involves problem-solving in the day-to-day management of their illness. They say,

"Patients with chronic conditions self-manage their illness. This fact is inescapable. Each day, patients decide what they are going to eat, whether they will exercise, and to what extent they will consume prescribed medications.... Patients are in control."

(Sound familiar? It reminds me of Chapter 5, **Respect** and **Be Honest**... **Relinquish Control!**) Bodenheimer, et al, feel that *teaching* needs to go way beyond just educating patients about their chronic illness. Teaching means we partner with our patients, collaborate with them, and teach them management and problem-solving skills (just like we discussed in **Humility**, to **Translate** our thought processes as well as our language.) Quality teaching uses all the skills we learn with the art of agape!

In another superb review, Daley (2001) discusses a case of a dissatisfied patient. The author points out that quality teaching, at every point in any healthcare encounter, improves patient satisfaction and patient outcome, as well as caregiver job satisfaction!

Another study by Laine et al (1996), the authors looked at surveys given to both patients and caregivers, asking them what is most important. Both patients and caregivers ranked "Clinical Skills" as the most important, but patients ranked "Information" as *second* most important! "Patients placed substantially greater value on effective communication of health-related information than did physicians." Again, we see that quality teaching is very important to patients.

These few papers are just a small sample of the studies that remind us about the importance of teaching to our patients. Teaching our patients does not just happen. Teaching takes time, and it takes effort. But, in the long run, it will pay off.

What if we, the caregiver, are a receptionist, an aide, or we just do not know much about pathophysiology? What can we teach?

When we do not know much about a disease or treatment or procedure, we should always be able to tell our patients *how* to get the information they crave. We may not know an answer, but we do know something about *the system*, and how it works. For example, when visitors are having trouble confronting a doctor or PA or nurse practitioner, I have shared with them the time that the caregiver makes rounds, and how best to catch them. I have suggested to family that they wave their arms and be animated when talking. I tell patients to prevent their doctor from leaving, until he or she provided answers they needed. I have explained to family the best times to call their primary caregivers, the best people in the office to ask for answers, and alternative ways to contact them. I suggest they write down all their questions. I have taught patients how to use the internet to find information they needed. And, I routinely ask that my patients get a second opinion, from pharmacists, their doctors or a specialist.

No one expects us to have all the answers. However, when we humbly admit our limitations, and teach what we *do* know about our hospital or office or clinic, we have cared for our patients with love.

When we teach with the art of agape, it's good for us, and great for our patients. And, it's the right thing to do.

**Summary: Patients crave information. The best teaching is done compassionately, respectfully, and with humility.**

# 21

# *We Are Individuals*

## Suppose I Am Not a "People Person"?

What does it mean to be a "people person"? Most of us assume that a "people person" is an extrovert … someone who is talkative or gregarious. Many of us might assume that behaving with the principles of agape, and improving our care-giving styles, demands that we be an extrovert, or that we change.

This is not true.

A "people person" is someone who focuses their attention on the other person. A "people person" is able to look at another person, listen to another person, and then imagine what life must be like for that other person. A "people person" has empathy, listens well, and allows the other person to be the focus of the attention. A "people person" behaves with agape.

There are many fine books on personality types. There are whole psychology departments devoted to the study of personality. There is a large section of the Diagnostic and Statistical Manual for Psychiatric Disorders devoted to personality disorders.

Interacting with agape does not depend on our personality.

Let us use a metaphor. Imagine that you are a tree. You are a tree that bears fruit. Agape is the soil in which you have your roots. Agape nourishes you. Agape fills you with life. Agape anchors you to the earth. Without agape, you are sick and lifeless, with very little fruit. As we are nourished with the love of agape, beautiful blossoms arise, and rich, life-giving fruit is borne. The fruit will be different for all of us … some of us give apples, some give peaches, some give figs. These fruits are gifts we give to people around us. Our compassion, our respect and our humility nourish us. The gifts we give to other people will be unique for each one of us. Yet, these are all wonderful gifts, for everyone we meet.

For example, let's discuss how we say "thank you." In the section on Humility and Admiration, we discussed how important it is to say, "Thank you." However, each one of us will say it differently, and we'll say it different ways with different patients.

Only *you* can determine which way is best for you.

One of us might smile broadly and bark out an enthusiastic, "Thanks!" Or, we might gently hold our patient's hand and quietly say, "I really appreciate your efforts." Maybe, depending on the patient, we might say, "Thanks very much for all the work you have done!" Or, perhaps a small respectful bow as we leave the room will indicate our thanks.

When agape underlies our motivations, we believe that saying "thanks" is the right thing to do. We want our patients to have a good experience. Agape fuels our desire for our patients to have a good experience. The *way* we give thanks is unique to us.

Let's take another example. How do we listen? As I mentioned, I like to *really* actively listen. I sometimes pace back and forth, stroke my chin, and act like Sherlock Holmes, nodding my head, and asking for more information. Other caregivers may simply sit quietly and look deeply into the eyes of their patient, nodding ever so gently. Another caregiver, perhaps someone who has never tried active listening, will repeat back each phrase their patient says, so as to demonstrate that their patient was heard. Another caregiver may say, "I am going to write while I listen, I hope you don't mind, and I will ask for clarification if I don't understand something. Is that okay with you?" This caregiver may nod a lot, and say, "Yes, I see," and "Tell me more," while they listen and write.

We listen actively and carefully because we act with agape. We want our patients to have a good experience. However, the way we listen, our *style* of listening, is unique to our personality.

All the suggestions and reminders contained in this book are meant to be *complementary* to our styles of interacting. Agape enriches and nourishes our personal ways of caring for other people.

You have read this book in the hope that you will become better at what you already do. These reminders help make our patients glad to have met us. Everyone who applies the principles of agape, and embodies these reminders, is allowed to act differently. However, their patients will feel the same: They will feel loved.

## Side Effects

As we get better with our art of agape for our patients, we will find ourselves happier. It is not possible to be unhappy while we smile. It's hard to be anxious or pressured when we are sincerely enjoying hearing about another person's life. Peace of mind, ease of living, organized thoughts, coherent actions, and pleasure in life will find you. These are some of the side effects of agape.

Agape will bring balance to our lives. "Work" will no longer be work, but merely another enjoyable way to pass the time. Work will become our way to make the world a better place. Work is our solace. We will enjoy our work. It will reduce the stress we find in other aspects of our lives.

A compassionate person will discover that compassion seeks him or her out. As we learn to walk in another person's shoes, so will everyone we meet find it easier to see our point of view, to walk in our shoes. Our soft touch will engender softness elsewhere in our lives. Our undistracted attention will allow others we meet to focus on us completely. Our whispers will be heard, and heard better than all our shouts.

These side effects are inevitable. They cannot be helped.

### Act, and the Thoughts Will Follow

In this book I have suggested ways to act. I have described behaviors. I have offered concrete, tangible, easily reproducible actions we can use in our clinical practice.

Since our actions are what our patients see and hear, our actions are what are important.

What if someone does not care? Suppose a caregiver says,

*"I don't feel any compassion for them ... they brought this illness on them self!"*

Or,

*"I don't care! So what if I'm rude, my patients are rude to me!"*

Or perhaps,

*"Why should I be humble? These patients know absolutely nothing about healthcare, and I've worked here for twenty years!"*

And you know what? At this stage, it does not matter what those caregivers might *feel*. But, it does matter how they *act*.

This idea, that we should *act* in a caring manner, is not new. Finestone and Conter (1994) published an essay in which they advocated an *acting* curriculum in professional training! These authors felt that, since complex feelings like empathy are difficult to teach, students should be taught to *act* empathic.

I agree! That's what it's all about: We need to *act* like we care.

When we *act* in a caring manner, when we act with agape, our patients are happier because of those *act*ions. And that is what our jobs are all about: making someone else feel better.

When we act with agape, sooner or later, our thoughts and feelings will follow our actions. Actions can shape our thoughts. Our behavior patterns will soon influence how we feel and think.

(If you want to know why, it's because of *cognitive dissonance*. We alluded to this on page 183. Cognitive dissonance is an uncomfortable feeling we have when things we *think or say* are very different from things we *do*. So long as we keep behaving with agape, cognitive dissonance will pull our thoughts and feelings into alignment with our actions. We *will* care.)

## A Loving Caregiver

One way that you can tell that you have "arrived," that is, that you are a truly loving caregiver, is when you defend your patients from criticisms of other caregivers. You have arrived when you give your patients the benefit of the doubt. You will embody and feel the principles of agape when you are *proud* that you are caring for them.

For example, let's say you are assigned to care for the nastiest, dirtiest most unpleasant patient. When you leave that patient, and tell your fellow caregivers good things about that patient, you will have found the art of agape. You will be a leader.

This is nicely summarized in an excerpt from *Chicken Soup for the Nurse's Soul:*

Definitely an untouchable!

The nurses at the station looked wide-eyed as this mound of humanity was wheeled by—each glancing nervously at my friend Bonnie, the head nurse. "Let this one not be mine, to admit, bathe and tend to..." was the pleading unspoken message from their inner concern.

One of the true marks of a leader, a consummate professional, is to do the unthinkable. To touch the untouchable. To tackle the impossible. Yes, it was Bonnie who said, "I want this patient for myself." Highly unusual for a head nurse—unconventional—but "the stuff" out of which human spirits thrive, heal and soar. (Naomi Rhode)

When this occurs to you, you will be a teacher of other caregivers. You'll share with your co-workers the joy of caring for people, no matter who they are or what circumstances landed them in your care. You will love your job and you will love your patients.

**Summary: Agape enriches and improves us. Agape helps improve our patients' lives as well as our lives.**

# References

Balzer-Riley, JW (1996). *Communications in Nursing*. Mosby: St. Louis.

Bartlett, EE (1988). Reducing the Malpractice Threat through Patient Communications. *Health Progress*. May, 1988: 63-66.

Bartlett, EE, Grayson, M, Barker, R, Levine, DM, Golden, A & Libber, S (1984). The Effects of Physician Communications Skills on Patient Satisfaction, Recall, and Adherence. *Journal of Chronic Diseases, 37* (9/10), 755-64.

Beckman, HB & Frankel, RM (1984). The Effect of Physician Behavior on Collection of Data. *Annals of Internal Medicine, 101* (5): 692-96.

Beckman, HB, Markakis, KM, Suchman, AL, & Frankel, RM (1994). The Doctor Patient Relationship and Malpractice. *Archives of Internal Medicine, 154*: 1365-70.

Bell, R & Krivich, MJ (2000). *How to Use Patient Satisfaction Data to Improve Healthcare Quality*. ASJ Quality Press: Milwaukee, WI, 19-32.

Berger, AS (2002). Arrogance Among Physicians. *Academic Medicine, 77* (2): 145-47.

Bodenheimer, T, Lorig, K, Holman, H, & Grumbach, K (2002). Patient Self Management of Chronic Disease in Primary Care. *JAMA, 288* (19), 2469-75.

Boothman, N (2000). *How to Make People Like You in 90 Seconds or Less*. Workman: NY.

Boudreaux, ED & O'Hea, EL (2004). Patient satisfaction in the Emergency Department: A review of the literature and implications for practice. *The Journal of Emergency Medicine, 26*(1): 13-26.

Caleel, RT (1986). *Surgeon!* Rawson Associates, NY. P. 37.

Canfield, J, Hansen, MJ, Mitchell-Autio, N, & Thieman, L (2000). *Chicken Soup for the Nurse's Soul.* Health Communications, Inc: Deerfield Beach, FL.

Coulehan, JL, Platt, FW, Egener, B, Frankel, R, Lin, CT, Lown, B, & Salazar, WH (2001). "Let Me See If I Have This Right…" Words That Help Build Empathy. *Annals of Internal Medicine, 135* (3), 221-27.

Cousins, N (1979). *Anatomy of an Illness.* Bantam Doubleday Dell: NY.

Covey, S (1990). *The Seven Habits of Highly Effective People.* Simon & Schuster: NY.

Daley, J (2001). A 58-Year-Old Woman Dissatisfied with Her Care. *JAMA, 285* (20), 2629-35.

Dingman, SK, Williams, M, Fosbinder, D, & Warnick, M (1999). Implementing a Caring Model to Improve Patient Satisfaction. *JONA, 29* (12): 30-37.

Doering, GT (1998). Patient Satisfaction in the Pre-Hospital Setting. *Emergency Medical Services, 27* (9): 69-74.

Engel, B (2001). *The Power of Apology.* John Wiley & Sons: NY.

Entman, SS (1994). The Relationship Between Malpractice Claims History and Subsequent Obstetric Care. *JAMA, 272* (20): 1588-91.

Farber, BA, Raskin, PM, & Brink, DC (eds.) (1998). *The Psychology of Carl Rogers.* Guilford Press: NY.

Finestone, HM & Conter, DB (1994). Acting in Medical Practice. *Lancet, 344,* Sept. 17: 801-02.

Friedman, SM, Daub, C, Cresci, K, & Keyser, R (1999). A Comparison of Job Satisfaction Among Nursing Assistants in Nursing Homes and the Program of All inclusive Care for the Elderly (PACE). *Gerontologist, 39* (4): 434-39.

Gawande, A (2002). *Complications.* Henry Holt: NY. Pp. 218-19.

Giannini, AJ, Tamulonis, D, Giannini, MC, Loiselle, RH, & Spirtos, G (1984). Defective Response to Social Cues in Mobius Syndrome. *Journal of Nervous and Mental Disorders. 172* (3): 174-75.

Godolphin, W, Towle, A, & McKendry, R (2001). Challenges in Family Practice Related to Informed and Shared Decision Making. *CMAJ, 165* (4): 434-35.

Gross, DA, Zyzanski, SJ, Borawski, EA, Cebul, RD, & Stange, KC (1998). Patient Satisfaction with Time Spent with Their Physician. *Journal of Family Practice, 47* (2): 133-37.

Henry, GL (2002). Preventing Malpractice Claims: The Power of Interpersonal Relationships. Talk given at ACEP Scientific Assembly, Seattle, WA. Oct, 2002.

Henry, GL & Sullivan, DJ (1997). *Emergency Medicine Risk Management.* ACEP: Dallas.

Hickson, GB, Clayton, EW, Entman, SS, Miller, CS, Githens, PB, Whetten-Goldstein, K, & Sloan, FA (1994). Obstetricians Prior Malpractice Experience and Patients' Satisfaction with Care. *JAMA, 272* (20): 1583-87.

Hostutler, JJ, Taft, SH, & Snyder, C (1999). Patient Needs in the Emergency Department: Nurses' and Pateints' Perceptions. *JONA 29* (1): 43050.

King, M, Novik, L, & Citrenbaum, C (1983). *Irresistible Communication: Creative Skills for the Health Professional.* WB Saunders: Philadelphia, PA. Pp. 24-25.

Kipp, KM (2001). Implementing Nursing Caring Standards in the Emergency Department. *JONA, 31* (2): 85-90.

Kuhr, S (1993). Mind Your Manners. *JEMS,* July 1993: 13-15.

Laine, C, Davidoff, F, Lewis, CE, Nelson, EC, Nelson, E, Kessler, RC, & Delbanco, TL (1996). Important Elements of Outpatient Care: A Comparison of Patients' and Physicians' Opinions. *Annals of Internal Medicine,* Vol. *125,* #8: 640-45.

Lang, F, Floyd, MR, & Beine, KL (2000). Clues to Patients' Explanations and Concerns About Their Illness: A Call for Active Listening. *Archives of Family Medicine, 9* : 222-27.

Larsen, KM & Smith, CK (1981). Assessment of Nonverbal Communication in the Patient- Physician Interview. *Journal of Family Practice.* 12: 481-88.

Levenson, RW, Ekman, P, & Friesen, WV (1990). Voluntary Facial Action Generates Emotion Specific Autonomic Nervous System Activity. *Psychophysiology.* 27 (4): 363-84.

Levinson, W, Gorawara-Bhat, R, & Lamb, J (2000). A Study of Patient Clues and Physician Responses in Primary Care and Surgical Settings. *JAMA, 284* (8): 1021-27.

Levinson, W & Roter, D (1993). The Effects of Two Continuing Medical Education Programs on Communication Skills. *Journal of General Internal Medicine*, 8: 318-24.

Levinson, W, Roter, DL, Mullolly, JP, Dull, VT, & Frankel, RM (1997). Physician Patient Communication. The Relationship with Malpractice Claims Among Primary Care Physicians and Surgeons. *JAMA, 277* (7): 553-59.

Lin, CT, Albertson, GA, Schilling, LM, Cyran, EM, Anderson, SN, Ware, L & Anderson, RJ (2001). Is Patients' Perceptions of Time Spent with the Physician a Determinant of Ambulatory Patient Satisfaction? *Archives of Internal Medicine, 161*: 1437-42.

Lipkin, M Jr (1996). Physician Patient Interaction in Reproductive Counseling. *Obstetrics and Gynecology. 88* (3 suppl): 31s-40s.

Little, P, Everitt, H, Williamson, I, Warner, G, Moore, M, Gould, C, Ferrier, K, & Payne, S (2001). Observational Study of Effect of Patient Centredness and Positive Approach on Outcomes of General Practice Consultations. *British Medical Journal, 323*, pp. 908-11.

Locailo, AR, Lawthers, AG, Brannan TA, Laird, NM, Hebert, LE, Peterson, LM Newhouse, JP, Weiler, PC, & Hiatt, HH (1991). Relation Between Malpractice Claims and Adverse Events Due to Negligence. *NEJM, 325*: 245-51.

London, O (1987). *Kill As Few Patients as Possible*. Ten Speed Press.

Maguire, P (2000). *Communication Skills for Doctors*. Arnold: London. Pp. 119-29.

Malloch, K, Sluyter, D, & Moore, N (2000). Relationship-Centered Care: Achieving True Value in Healthcare. *JONA, 30* (7/8): 379-85.

Mangels, LS (1991). Tips from Doctors Who Have Never Been Sued. *Medical Economics*, February 18, 1991: 56-64.

Markakis, KM, Beckman, HB, Suchman, A, & Frankel, RM (2000). The Path to Professionalism: Cultivating Humanistic Values and Attitudes in Residency Training. *Academic Medicine, 75*: 141-50.

Marvel, MK, Epstein, RM, Flowers, K, & Beckman, HB (1999). Soliciting the Patient's Agenda. *JAMA, 281* (3): 283-87.

Mehrabian, A & Williams, M (1969). Nonverbal Concomitants of Perceived and Intended Persuasiveness. *Journal of Personality and Social Psychology. 13*: 37-58.

Morse, JM (2000). On Comfort and Comforting. *American Journal of Nursing,100* (9): 34-38.

Moyle, S (1999). Health Care Practice and the Minimization of Patient Medical Litigation. *Australian Health Review 22* (3) 44-55.

Nelson, AM (1997). *Improving Patient Satisfaction Now.* Aspen Publishers: Gaithersburg, MD.

Neuwirth, ZE (1997). Physician Empathy—Should We Care? *The Lancet, 350*: 606.

Nolin, CE (1995). Malpractice Claims, Patient Communication, and Critical Paths: A Lawyer's Perspective. *Quality Management in Health Care, 3* (2): 65-70.

Northouse, LL & Northouse, PG (1998). *Health Communication.* Appleton&Lange: Stamford, CT. Pp. 140-41.

*Patch Adams* (1998). Universal Studios.

Probst, JC, Greenhouse, DL, & Selassie, AW (1997). Patient and Physician Satisfaction with an Outpatient Care Visit. *Journal of Family Practice 45* (5): 418-25.

Purtilo, R & Haddad, Amy (1996). Health Professional and Patient Interaction. WBSaunders: Philadelphia, PA. Pp. 190-91.

Redelmeier, DA, Molin, JP, & Tibshirani, RJ (1995). A Randomized Trial of Compassionate Care for the Homeless in an Emergency Department. *The Lancet, 345*: 1131-34.

Rhoades, DR, McFarland, KF, Finch, WH, & Johnson, AO (2001). Speaking and Interruptions During Primary Care Office Visits. *Family Medicine, 33* (7): 528-32.

Roter, DL & Hall, JA (1993). *Doctors Talking with Patients/Patients Talking with Doctors.* Auburn House: Westport, CT.

Roter, DL, Hall, JA, Kern, DE, Barker, LR, Cole, KA, & Roca, RP (1995). Improving Physicians' Interviewing Skills and Reducing Patients' Emotional Distress. *Archives of Internal Medicine, 155*: 1877-84.

Roter, DL, Stewart, M, Putnam, SM, Lipkin, M Jr., Stiles, W, & Inui, TS (1997). Communication Patterns of Primary Care Physicians. *JAMA, 277* (4): 350-56.

Schuster PM (2000). *Communication: The Key to the Therapeutic Relationship.* FADavis: Philadelphia, PA. P. 108.

Shapiro RS, Simpson, DE, Lawrence, SL, Talsky, AM, Sobocinski, KA, & Schiedermayer, DL (1989). A Survey of Sued and Non-sued Physicians and Suing Patients. *Archives of Internal Medicine, 149*: 2190-96.

Sherer, M & Rogers, RW (1980). Effects of Therapist's Nonverbal Communication on Rated Skill and Effectiveness. *Journal of Clinical Psychology, 36* (3): 696-700.

Shugars, DA, DiMatteo, MR, Hays, RD, Cretin, S, & Johnson, JD (1990). Professional Satisfaction Among California Dentists. *Journal of Dental Education, 54* (11): 661-69.

Smith, RC, Lyles, JS, Mettler, JA, Marshall, AA, Van Egeren, LF, Stoffelmayr, BE, Osborn, GG, & Shebroe, V (1995). A Strategy for Improving Patient Satisfaction by the Intensive Training of Residents in Psychosocial Medicine: A Controlled, Randomized Study. *Academic Medicine, 70* (8) 729-32.

Spiro, H, McCrea Curnen, MG, Peschel, E. a& St. James, D (1993). *Empathy and the Practice of Medicine.* Yale University Press: New Haven.

Stewart, M, Brown, JB, Weston, WW, McWhinney, IR, McWilliam, CL, & Freeman, TR (1995). *Patient Centered Medicine*: Sage Publications: Thousand Oaks, CA.

Strauss, RW & Strauss, SF (1997). Conflict Management. In Salluzzo, RF et al (eds.), *Emergency Department Management.* Mosby, NY.

Strecher, VJ (1983). Improving Physician Patient Interactions: A Review. *Patient Counseling and Health Education, 4* (3): 129-36.

Suchman, AL, Markakis, K, Beckman, HB, & Frankel, R (1997). A Model of Empathic Communication in the Medical Interview. *JAMA, 277* (8): 678-82.

Thom, DH (2001). Physician Behaviors That Predict Patient Trust. *Journal of Family Practice, 50* (4): 323-28.

Virshup, BB, Oppenberg, AA, & Coleman, MM (1999). Strategic Risk Management: Reducing Malpractice Claims Through More Effective Patient Doctor Communication. *American Journal of Medical Quality, 14* (4): 153-59.

Weston, WW (2001). Informed and Shared Decision Making: The Crux of Patient Centered Care. *CMAJ, 165* (4): 438-39.

White, AA (1999). Compassionate Patient Care and Personal Survival. *Clinical Orthopedics, 361*: 250-60.

Zinn, W (1993). The Empathic Physician. *Archives of Internal Medicine, 153*: 306-12.

# Index

# About the Author

$S$cott Louis Diering, M.D., was born and raised in New Jersey. The second of three children, he grew up ever-curious and thirsting for knowledge and education. He graduated Rutgers College in New Brunswick, NJ in 1983, and earned a Master's degree in clinical psychology from UNC-Greensboro in 1986. He worked with developmentally disabled adults while preparing for medical school. He graduated Wake Forest University School of Medicine in 1992. After being accepted in, but not integrating well with, a neurosurgical residency, he completed a residency in emergency medicine, at the University of Michigan, in 1998. Dr. Diering now lives and practices emergency medicine in Maryland and Washington, DC. He is also on faculty at the International University of the Health Sciences.

The father of three children, he is always seeking ways to make the world a better place. If you have any suggestions on how to make *Love Your Patients!* or healthcare better, please let him know.

stories@loveyourpatients.org
Message line: (301) 620 1933 or 1 (866) 227 8808 pin 7804
Visit our website: www.loveyourpatients.org
Feel free to email him: diering@loveyourpatients.org

*Who are you? What are you? Where are you?*

Tell us your story! Are you a patient? A family member or friend of a patient? That's great ... tell us all about your experiences! We want to hear from you!

Are you a nurse? A doctor? A technician? An aide? Let us know about what your life in healthcare is like!

Email: stories@loveyourpatients.org

Phone the message line: 301 620 1933
or 1 866 227 8808 pin 7801

Mail it to us:   Love Your Patients!
                 99 Siegel Ct.
                 Frederick, Maryland 21702

Or visit our website, www.loveyourpatients.org
And go to the "Tell us about you!" section.